Dear Richard,
With thanks to Peerless
for introducing us to each other.
—Joel,

WOMEN AT THE SEDER
A PASSOVER HAGGADAH
הגדה של פסח

JOEL B. WOLOWELSKY

KTAV PUBLISHING HOUSE
930 NEWARK AVENUE
JERSEY CITY, NJ 07306

Library of Congress Cataloging-in-Publication Data

Haggadah. English & Hebrew.
  Women at the seder : a Passover Haggadah / [commentary by]
Joel B. Wolowelsky.
    p. cm.
  ISBN 0-88125-869-5
  1. Haggadot--Texts. 2. Seder--Liturgy--Texts. 3. Judaism
--Liturgy--Texts. 4. Jewish women--Religious life. 5. Haggadah.
I. Wolowelsky, Joel B. II. Title.
BM674.643.W65 2004
296.4'5371--dc22   2004019273

Cover design by Enya Keshet

Typesetting by Jerusalem Typesetters

Manufactured in the United States of America

Published by
KTAV Publishing House, Inc.
930 Newark Avenue
Jersey City, NJ 07306
Email: orders@ktav.com
www.ktav.com
(201) 963-9524
Fax (201) 963-0102

INTRODUCTION

Women at the Seder: A Passover Haggadah is a celebration of one of the great transformations of the Torah community during this past century: the emergence of women from the privacy of their home "tents" to the public arena of the synagogue and *beit medrash*, without abandoning in any way their central traditional role as the cornerstone of the home and family.

In many ways, this transformation parallels developments in the more general secular society. Women have entered the universities and professions, learning to balance new and traditional responsibilities. In the Torah world, religious adolescent women are expected to continue in yeshivah high schools and post-graduate seminaries, often spending a year away from home in Israel. For people who can remember the times when it was natural for boys in a family to attend a yeshivah while their sisters went to public school, this is truly amazing. Today we take for granted that women will not only learn Torah at advanced levels, but also develop professional halakhic competence. We have *to'anot rabbaniyot* practicing before the Israeli Rabbinic Courts, and *yo'atsot halakhah* addressing personal questions of *niddah* and *taharat hamishpaha*. Women head institutions of college-level Jewish studies and publish articles on Torah subjects. The pace of all of this is accelerating, and it is invigorating to watch and appreciate.

Women at the Seder is a traditional Haggadah whose commentary honors these achievements. The Rabbis had long ago acknowledged that it was in the merit of our righteous women that Israel was redeemed from slavery. The Passover *seder* – our home celebration of our national liberation – seems an appropriate place to acknowledge and honor women's expanded role in our public as well as private religious life.

In creating the commentary, I first collected rabbinic comments on women associated with the Exodus along with a discussion of those relevant halakhot that apply to women. Then I added *divrei Torah* by women for the *seder*, trying to be representative rather than exhaustive. I have included *divrei Torah* from two contemporary teachers of Torah whose public Torah *sheurim* have reached thousands of people, Nechama Leibowitz *zt"l* and Avivah Gottlieb Zornberg *talit"a*. I have incorporated some of the creative suggestions of Yael Levine, and some *divrei Torah* from previously published comments by women on the secondary, college and post-graduate levels, including the *Yeshivat Ramaz Likrat Shabbat Haggadah;* the *Columbia University Beit Midrash Haggadah;* the *Celebration of the Haggadah* of The Women's Beit Midrash, and *Kolekh*, the publication of the *Forum Nashim Datiyot*. I invited women I know who are involved in *hinukh* and their friends to contribute some of the *divrei Torah* they have shared with others at their own *sedarim*. Ariana Nehmad provided the illustrations of the "four daughters." In a generation, it should seem quaint that it was noteworthy that women's *divrei Torah* constituted a significant part of a Haggadah commentary. That will be cause for yet additional rejoicing, as women's contributions on all levels of Torah scholarship will have become even more commonplace.

I have also included references to two of the major orientating experiences of the past century, the Holocaust and, at the other pole, the reestablishment of the State of Israel. In addition, even though this is an Ashkenazic Haggadah, I have from time to time taken note of Sephardic variations and customs. I did so for two reasons. First, the end of the relative isolation of our Ashkenazic and Sephardic communities that marks our contemporary religious society is itself a cause for additional celebration. Second, it reminds us that while not every variation in custom or ritual suggestion that we encounter may be halakhically acceptable, not having seen something in our own homes does not necessarily make it illegitimate. Indeed, we have much to learn from being open to additional legitimate ways of expressing our religious commitment.

I am grateful to all those whose thoughts appear in this commentary, and the many colleagues and friends who kept suggesting additional sources and corrections to me as they saw various earlier drafts. In addition, I want to acknowledge and thank my publisher, Mr. Bernie Scharfstein of Ktav Publishing House, for his good advice, his continued confidence and, most importantly, his friendship. The beautiful cover artwork is an original design by noted Israeli artist Enya Keshet, represented in the United States by Bleema Posner of Rimonim Booksellers, Englewood, New Jersey. Raphaël Freeman at Jerusalem Typesetting in Israel fashioned the handsome design of the Haggadah and Ricky Fleischer set the actual text with great professionalism and patience regarding my various last-minute corrections.

Most importantly, I am grateful to the members of my extended family who year after year, decade after decade, made the *seder* one of the highlights of my personal religious life: the Wolowelskys, Rosenblatts and Weinbaums; the Fishmans, Mohls and Finkels; and the Kriegers and Reichs. Just as we were worthy to perform it, so may we be worthy to do so in the future, in good health and family solidarity.

Joel B. Wolowelsky

WOMEN AT THE SEDER
A PASSOVER HAGGADAH
הגדה של פסח

עֶרֶב פֶּסַח

הבכורים מתענים בערב פסח. ונוהגים להשתתף בסעודת
מצוה, כגון סיום מסכת, ולהיפטר מן הצום.

תְּחִינוֹת לְפֶסַח

פקח עיניך וראה, עפן דיינע אויגן ליבער גאט, און זעה די מיהע
פון דיין טייעד פאלק, וויפל מיהע זיי האבין צו דערהאלטן
דיינע מצות, וואס דו האסט זיי גיבאטן צו טאן אין דעם חודש
ניסן, צו פאר שטערן דעם חמץ פון זייער שטוב, און עסן
מצות אלע זיבן טעג פון פסח. ווי גרויס און שווער עס קומט
זיי אן, מחמת די אייגעניש פון זייער פרנסה, אבער זיי האלטן
דיין באפעל, און היטן דיינע מצות. דערום ליבער גאט שיק
איין שפע וברכה צו אלע יידן, און זאלסט אונז היטן מיט דיין
הייליגקייט, אז מיר זאלן ניט חלילה נכשל ווערן אין איסור
חמץ און פסח, און עס זאל אונז דער הייליגער יו"ט פסח גרינג
אנקומען, און מיר זאלין חלילה ניט דארפן אנקומען צו איין
מתנת בשר ודם, אמן.

Fast of the first-born

It would seem that first-born daughters should also have to fast on Erev Pesah, as they too were saved from the plague that killed all the first-born of Egypt. Some hold that opinion, but the general custom is that only the males fast (*Shulhan Arukh Orah Hayim* 470). The reason is that the Jewish males were not saved out of their own merit, but because of God's grace. The Jewish females, however, were saved through their own merit – "It was through the merit of the righteous women of that generation that the Jews were saved from Egypt" (*TB Sotah* 11b) – and therefore need not fast (*Ma'ase Rokeah*).

Rabbi Ovadiah Yosef maintains that nowadays we should follow the prevailing custom of their not fasting, especially since the males exempt themselves from fasting by attending a *siyum* or similar "festive" meal. Nonetheless, he adds, if without excessive effort the female first-born can attend such a meal, it is certainly most proper that she do so (*Yabia Yosef* 3:25).

The Seder Plate

The *zero'a* (meat) and egg on the *seder* plate

EREV PESAH

*The first-born must fast on Erev Pesah. However, the general custom is
for them to exempt themselves from the fast by attending a festive meal,
such as one celebrating the completion of a* masekhet *of Talmud.*

THE SEDER TABLE

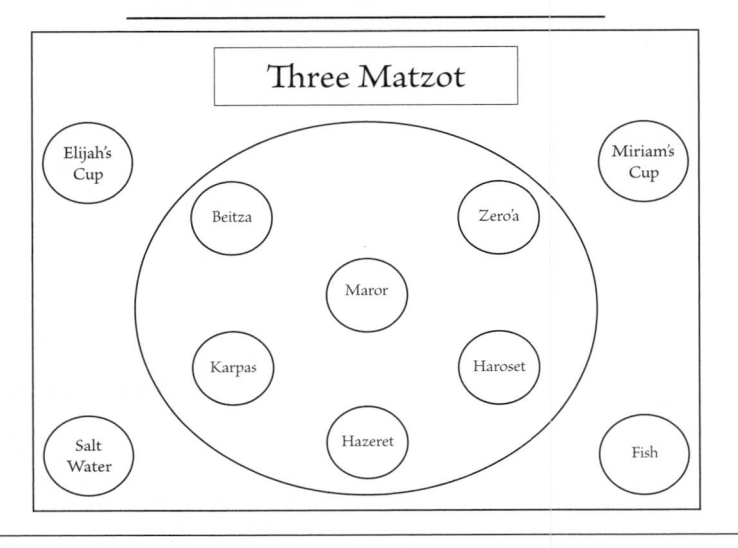

Three Matzot

Elijah's Cup

Miriam's Cup

Beitza

Zero'a

Maror

Karpas

Haroset

Salt Water

Hazeret

Fish

---

are usually thought to remind us of the Paschal and Hagiga sacrifices, respectively. But some seven centuries ago Rabbi Eleazer of Worms quoted Rav Shrira Gaon that they are reminders of the two leaders, Moses and Aaron, sent by God to the Jews when they were in Egypt. He then adds, there are those who add a fish item, the three foods thus commemorating Moses, Aaron, and Miriam, as the prophet Micah wrote, "I brought you up from the land of Egypt, I redeemed you from the house of bondage, and I sent before you Moses, Aaron, and Miriam" (*Micah* 6:4). These three cooked items correspond to the three types of food that the people of Israel will eat in the Messianic times: fish, corresponding to the leviathan; the egg corresponding to *ziz* (an

enormous bird); and meat, corresponding to *shor ha-bar* (behemoth) (*Ma'ase Rokeah*, number 59).

Fish at the *seder* has another association with the heroines of the Exodus. When the Jewish women would go to draw water, God arranged for small fish to fill up half their jugs. The women cooked the fish, which increased the husband's sexual potency, washed and fed their husbands in the field and encouraged them to have children – even in those hard times. Thus, says Rabbi Avira in introducing the story, "It was in the merit of the righteous women of that generation that the Jews were redeemed from Egypt" (*BT Sota* 11b).

Whether the *seder* plate be creatively redesigned to accommodate the fish, as Yael

אן אין זכות פון מרים הנביאה ע"ה: אדוני, גדענק אונז ליבער גאט אין זכות וואס זיא האט פאר דיר שירה געזאגט מיט די וויבער ווען די יידן זיינען אויף דעם ים געגאנגען אזוי ווי אין פסוק שטייט: "ותקח מרים הנביאה, אחות אהרון, את התוף בידה, ותצאנה כל הנשים אחריה בתופים ובמחולות, ותען להם מרים: 'שירו לה' כי גאה גאה סוס ורוכבו רמה בים'. דאס איז טייטש, מרים הנביאה די שוועסטער פון אהרון האט גענומען די פוק אין האנד, זענען ארויס געגאנגען אלע וויבער נאך מיט פוקין און כלי זמר האט מרים צו זיי געשריגן:"זינגט צו גאט דען ער האט געטאן הערשן, דעם פערד מיט זיין רייטער האט ער געוואורפן אין ים." אזוי זאלן מיר זוכה זיין צו זאגן שירה מיט אלע נשים צדקניות ווען משיח וועט קומען במהרה בימינו, אמן.

אֱלוֹהַּ אָהוּב

אֱלוֹהַּ אָהוּב, אָנָּא פְּקַח אֶת עֵינֶיךָ,
וּרְאֵה בָּעֳנִי עַמְּךָ, הוּא צֹאנֶךָ.
בְּנִיסָן מִמִּצְרַיִם גָּאַלְתָּ אָבוֹת,
וּמֵאָז בִּמְסִירוּת מְקַיְּמִים הֵם מִצְווֹת.
כֹּה דַּלָּה מִחְיָתָם, כֹּה גְּדוֹלָה טִרְחָתָם,
וּבְכָל זֹאת עוֹשִׂים אֶת אֲשֶׁר צִוִּיתָם.
לְכָל הַיְּהוּדִים שְׁלַח נָא שֶׁפַע בְּרָכָה,
הֵן הִשְׁבַּתְּנוּ חָמֵץ מֵחַצְרוֹת קָדְשֶׁךָ.
חֻקֵּי חַג-הַפֶּסַח מַלֵּא בְּיָדָם,
שֶׁלֹּא יִצְטָרְכוּ לְמַתְּנַת בָּשָׂר-וָדָם.

אַחַר הַנִּסִּים

אַחַר הַנִּסִּים שֶׁקָּרוּ עַל הַיָּם
וְאַחַר שִׁירָה, אָז יָצְאָה לָהּ מִרְיָם
אֲחוֹת אַהֲרֹן, בְּיָדָהּ הָיָה תֹף,
וַתֵּצֶאנָה נָשִׁים אַחֲרֶיהָ לַחוֹף.
שִׁירוּ לַה', כִּי גָאָה גָּאָה!
שָׁרָה מִרְיָם וְקוֹלָהּ שָׁם רָעַם,
שִׁירוּ לַה', הַמְּלוּכָה לוֹ נָאָה,
סוּס וְרֹכְבוֹ רָמָה בַיָּם!
כְּשֶׁמָּשִׁיחַ צִדְקֵנוּ יָבֹא, בִּמְהֵרָה,
תֵּצֶאנָה נָשִׁים אֶת פָּנָיו לְקַבֵּל.
כְּמִרְיָם — כֵּן נָשֵׁינוּ, זְקֵנָה וּצְעִירָה,
טְהוֹרוֹת וְזַכּוֹת, בִּזְכוּתָן נִגָּאֵל!
כְּמוֹ נְשׁוֹת הֶעָבָר בְּיַם-סוּף, עַל הַחוֹף,
תְּנַעֲמְנָה לַבָּא בְּזִמְירוֹת וּבְתֹף.

TKHINES FOR PEYSEKH

Pekakh Eynekha u-re-eh: Open Your eyes, beloved God, and see the efforts of Your dear people. How hard they try to keep during the month of Nissan the *mitsvos* which You commanded them: to rid their houses of *khometz* and to eat *matzos* all seven days of *Peysekh*. How difficult it is for them because of their meager income. But they keep Your commandments and observe the *mitzvos*. Therefore, beloved God, send Your beneficence and blessing to all Jews; protect us with Your holiness that we should not trespass the prohibition of *khometz* on *Peysekh*, and may the holy *yontev* of *Peysekh* be easy for us, and may we not be forced to take the gifts of others.

Now, dear God, remember for our sakes the merit of the prophetess Miryom who praised You in song along with other Jewish women when the Jews crossed the Sea. As the posuk *(Ex. 15:20–21)* states: "*Vatikakh Miryom ha-neviyo akhos Aharon es ha-tof be-yodo va-tetseno akhareho be-supim u-vimkholos. Va-ta-an lohem Miryom: Shiru lashem ki ga-o ga-a, sus ve-rokhvo rama vayom*" – which means: "When Miryom the prophetess, the sister of Aharon, took the drum in her hand, all the women gathered around her with drums and instruments. Then Miryom called out: 'Sing to God who lorded over horses and their riders, for He threw them into the sea.'" So let us be worthy to sing Your praises along with all the righteous women when *Moshiakh* comes. May he arrive soon and in our time. Amen.

Levine suggests (*All the Women Followed Her*), or the fish is simply placed on a small dish somewhere on the table, it stimulates questions and provides an opportunity to relate the contributions of "the righteous women" to our past and future liberation.

Miriam's Cup

With the current focus on women's contributions to the historical Jewish community, some have expanded the traditional custom of sparking children's questions to include "Miriam's Cup" – a goblet of pure water placed on the table so that the story of "Miriam's Well" can be told in response to the question about its significance. The "well" was actually a rock that accompanied the Jews and miraculously flowed on demand during their forty years in the desert (*Midrash Tanhuma Bemidbar 2*).

Tkhines for Peysekh

Tkhines are a folk Yiddish literary form through which European women poured out their hearts to God when lighting candles each Friday or holiday night, on

סֵדֶר הַדְלָקַת נֵרוֹת

בָּרוּךְ אַתָּה יְיָ, אֱלֹהֵינוּ מֶלֶךְ הָעוֹלָם, אֲשֶׁר קִדְּשָׁנוּ בְּמִצְוֹתָיו, וְצִוָּנוּ לְהַדְלִיק נֵר שֶׁל (בשבת: שֶׁל שַׁבָּת וְ) יוֹם טוֹב.

יש נוהגות להוסיף כאן:

בָּרוּךְ אַתָּה יְיָ, אֱלֹהֵינוּ מֶלֶךְ הָעוֹלָם, שֶׁהֶחֱיָנוּ וְקִיְּמָנוּ וְהִגִּיעָנוּ לַזְּמַן הַזֶּה.

בִּרְכַּת יְלָדִים

לבת:
יְשִׂמֵךְ אֱלֹהִים כְּשָׂרָה,
רִבְקָה, רָחֵל וְלֵאָה:

לבן:
יְשִׂמְךָ אֱלֹהִים
כְּאֶפְרַיִם וְכִמְנַשֶּׁה:

---

the Shabbat when the new month was announced, and at other special occasions. These two paragraphs were taken from, respectively, the *Tkhine Mikro Koydesh* (Lemberg) and the *Shas Tkhine* (Bilgoray), both published a century ago. They were selected and translated into English by Zelda Kahan Newman, using standard Yiddish transliteration. Avner Taler composed the Hebrew adaptation.

Sheheheyanu at Candle Lighting
Many *poskim* (e.g., R. Yaakov Emden, *Responsum 10*; R. Moshe Sternbuch, *Haggadah Moadim u-Zemanim*, p. 48) object to *Sheheheyanu* being said at candle lighting time instead of *Kiddush*. Others (e.g., *Mishnah Berurah* 263:5, n. 2; *Arukh HaShulhan Yoreh Deah* 263:12) feel that one need not object forcefully to the practice; it is a long-standing custom and, while the blessing

should relate to *kedushat hayom*, the holiness of the day itself (which begins only at night), the candles are usually lit very close to night.

On Shabbat, there are two customs regarding whether the blessing on the candles is said before or after lighting them (*Shulhan Arukh Orah Hayim* 263:5, Ramo's gloss). Generally, a *berakhah* should be said before performing the mitzvah and many therefore light the candles after saying the blessing. (However, if one sees saying the blessing (rather than lighting the candles) as constituting early acceptance of Shabbat, one can light the candles after saying the blessing only if she made a specific declaration that Shabbat not begin until after the candles are lit.) Those who say the *berakhah* after lighting the candles consider the act over which they are saying the blessing to be deriving pleasure from the light of the candles. They

---

CANDLE LIGHTING

On Friday night add the words in brackets:

Blessed are You, Lord, our God, King of the universe, who has sanctified us with His mitzvot and commanded us to light the [Shabbat and] Festival candles.

Some women add at this time:

Blessed are You, Lord, our God, King of the universe, who has granted us life, sustained us, and enabled us to reach this occasion.

BLESSING THE CHILDREN

For sons:	*For daughters:*
May God make you like Ephraim and Menasseh.	May God make you like Sarah, Rebecca, Rachel and Leah.

---

therefore cover their eyes after lighting the candles so as not to benefit from their light until after the blessing is said.

Rabbanit Baila Falk, wife of the author of the *Drishah*, maintained that on holidays, when lighting the candles is permitted, there is no reason to say the blessing after the kindling and it therefore should be said before the kindling (*end of introduction to the Drishah*). *Magen Avraham* (*Shulhan Arukh Orah Hayim* 263:5, n. 12) dismisses her ruling, quoting R. Eliezer's aphorism that "there is no wisdom among women" (*TB Yoma* 66b). *Dagul Merevava* (*ibid.*) rules that the law is in accordance with her position.

Those following her ruling should say *Sheheheyanu* after the candles are lit (if they do not defer saying it until *Kiddush* is said), as it relates to the *kedushat hayom*, which begins with the lighting (*Haggadah Mo'adim u-Zemanim*, p. 48). On Shabbat, one can light candles without accepting Shabbat early by making an explicit *tenai* (condition) at the time of lighting. This cannot be done if *Sheheheyanu* is said, as there is no *kedushat hayom* if the holiday has not begun.

Like Rachel and Leah

Siddurim generally mention the four Matriarchs in the blessing for a daughter, but Rabbi Yehudah Herzl Henkin (*Kolekh* no. 9) points out that this formulation is first found in 19th-century *siddurim* and is not exactly parallel to the son's blessing, which is based on the verse, "By this you shall bless Israel, saying 'God make you like Ephraim and like Menasseh'" (*Genesis* 48:20). He suggests the blessing for daughters should also be based on a biblical verse: "All the people that were in the gate, and all the elders, said, 'We are witnesses. The Lord make the woman that is come into your

יְבָרֶכְךָ יְיָ וְיִשְׁמְרֶךָ.

יָאֵר יְיָ פָּנָיו אֵלֶיךָ וִיחֻנֶּךָּ.

יִשָּׂא יְיָ פָּנָיו אֵלֶיךָ וְיָשֵׂם לְךָ שָׁלוֹם.

הַמַּלְאָךְ הַגֹּאֵל אֹתִי מִכָּל רָע יְבָרֵךְ אֶת הַנְּעָרִים, וְיִקָּרֵא בָהֶם שְׁמִי וְשֵׁם אֲבֹתַי אַבְרָהָם וְיִצְחָק, וְיִדְגּוּ לָרֹב בְּקֶרֶב הָאָרֶץ:

קַדֵּשׁ

מוזגים לכל המסובים כוס ראשונה

בשבת מתחילים כאן:

בלחש: וַיְהִי עֶרֶב וַיְהִי בֹקֶר

יוֹם הַשִּׁשִּׁי, וַיְכֻלּוּ הַשָּׁמַיִם וְהָאָרֶץ וְכָל־צְבָאָם: וַיְכַל אֱלֹהִים בַּיּוֹם הַשְּׁבִיעִי, מְלַאכְתּוֹ אֲשֶׁר עָשָׂה, וַיִּשְׁבֹּת בַּיּוֹם הַשְּׁבִיעִי, מִכָּל־מְלַאכְתּוֹ אֲשֶׁר עָשָׂה: וַיְבָרֶךְ אֱלֹהִים אֶת־יוֹם הַשְּׁבִיעִי, וַיְקַדֵּשׁ אֹתוֹ, כִּי בוֹ שָׁבַת מִכָּל־מְלַאכְתּוֹ, אֲשֶׁר־בָּרָא אֱלֹהִים לַעֲשׂוֹת:

---

house like Rachel and like Leah, which two did build the house of Israel'" (*Ruth* 4:11).

Kiddush

In the Babylonian Talmud (*Pesahim* 105b), Rabbi Nahman bar Yitzhak teaches the obligation to recite *Kiddush* applies as soon as Shabbat or Yom Tov begins. He says: "I am neither a sage nor a preacher nor a great scholar, but I study the traditions in my possession and organize the *halakhot*, and this is why they teach in the *beit midrash* according to my opinion." R. Nachman stresses that his answer is not the result of any complex thought process or erudite innovation, but rather is based on a long-standing tradition with which he is familiar. This message symbolically elucidates

the meaning of the *Kiddush*. The *Kiddush* is a kind of coronation; we crown the current day by citing God's involvement in history. Through reciting the *Kiddush*, a Jew links the current sanctified day with the entire course of the history of the Jewish people (Malka Puterkovsky, *A Celebration of the Haggadah*, The Women's Beit Midrash).

The obligation to say *Kiddush* each Friday night is at a biblical level for both men and women, even though *Kiddush* is a time-bound commandment from which women are generally exempt. Inasmuch as they share a common obligation, men can fulfill their obligation in *Kiddush* by hearing a woman say it (*Shulhan Arukh Orah Hayim* 271:2). However, the nature of the obligation of *Kiddush* on a holiday is a matter

May God bless you and watch over you.
May God shine His face towards you and show you favor.
May God turn His face towards you and grant you peace.
The angel who has redeemed me from all evil should bless the children, and let my name be named in them, and the name of my fathers Abraham and Isaac, and let them grow into a multitude in the midst of the earth.

KADESH

The first cup of wine is poured.

On Friday night begin with the following paragraph:
Silently: It was evening and it was morning
The sixth day. The heavens and the earth and all their hosts were completed. On the seventh day God finished His work which He had made, and He rested on the seventh day from all His work which He had made. God blessed the seventh day and made it holy, for on it He rested from all His work which God had created and done.

---

of some dispute. Rambam (Maimonides) writes that *Kiddush* on the eve of a holiday is the same as that on Friday night, as all the holidays are considered "*Shabbatot laShem*" (*Mishne Torah, Hilkhot Shabbat* 29:18), echoing the Midrash (*Mehilta Yitro* 7). Nonetheless, many authorities consider this an *asmakhta*, that is, a rhetorical "proof" for a rabbinic decision. While the majority of *Rishonim* seem to hold that it is a Torah obligation, the majority of *Aharonim* hold that it is rabbinic (*R. Ovadiah Yosef, Hazon Ovadiah* 1:2).

This dispute impacts on the question of a woman's obligation in *Kiddush* at the *seder*. Women are not excused from any Shabbat obligation, even if it is time-bound; such would not necessarily be the case for holiday time-bound mitzvot. Two main rea-sons are suggested for their being obligated from the Torah if the men are. First, the fact that the holidays are "*Shabbatot laShem*" means that the rules of Shabbat apply here too. Second, paralleling the reasoning in Shabbat mitzvot, women are obligated in *Kiddush* and matzah even though they are time-bound obligations because they are obliged in the prohibitions of *hametz* on that night. On the other hand, if the obligation for men is rabbinic, women would also be obligated either because the exemption from time-bound mitzvot applies only to Torah obligations, not rabbinic ones, or because the rabbinic obligation in the four cups of wine encompasses *Kiddush*.

People can remain quiet and fulfill their own obligation to say a blessing by listening to the blessing said by another individual

ביו"ט מתחילים כאן:

סַבְרִי מָרָנָן וְרַבָּנָן וְרַבּוֹתַי:

בָּרוּךְ אַתָּה יְיָ, אֱלֹהֵינוּ מֶלֶךְ הָעוֹלָם, בּוֹרֵא פְּרִי הַגָּפֶן:

בָּרוּךְ אַתָּה יְיָ, אֱלֹהֵינוּ מֶלֶךְ הָעוֹלָם, אֲשֶׁר בָּחַר בָּנוּ מִכָּל־עָם, וְרוֹמְמָנוּ מִכָּל־לָשׁוֹן, וְקִדְּשָׁנוּ בְּמִצְוֹתָיו, וַתִּתֶּן־לָנוּ יְיָ אֱלֹהֵינוּ בְּאַהֲבָה (בשבת: שַׁבָּתוֹת לִמְנוּחָה וּ)מוֹעֲדִים לְשִׂמְחָה, חַגִּים וּזְמַנִּים לְשָׂשׂוֹן. אֶת־יוֹם (בשבת: הַשַּׁבָּת הַזֶּה, וְאֶת־יוֹם) חַג הַמַּצּוֹת הַזֶּה. זְמַן חֵרוּתֵנוּ, (בשבת: בְּאַהֲבָה,) מִקְרָא קֹדֶשׁ, זֵכֶר לִיצִיאַת מִצְרָיִם. כִּי בָנוּ בָחַרְתָּ וְאוֹתָנוּ קִדַּשְׁתָּ מִכָּל־הָעַמִּים. (בשבת: וְשַׁבָּת) וּמוֹעֲדֵי קָדְשֶׁךָ (בשבת: בְּאַהֲבָה וּבְרָצוֹן) בְּשִׂמְחָה וּבְשָׂשׂוֹן הִנְחַלְתָּנוּ. בָּרוּךְ אַתָּה יְיָ, מְקַדֵּשׁ (בשבת: הַשַּׁבָּת וְ)יִשְׂרָאֵל וְהַזְּמַנִּים:

במוצאי שבת מוסיפים את שתי הברכות הבאות:

בָּרוּךְ אַתָּה יְיָ, אֱלֹהֵינוּ מֶלֶךְ הָעוֹלָם, בּוֹרֵא מְאוֹרֵי הָאֵשׁ:

בָּרוּךְ אַתָּה יְיָ, אֱלֹהֵינוּ מֶלֶךְ הָעוֹלָם, הַמַּבְדִּיל בֵּין קֹדֶשׁ לְחֹל, בֵּין אוֹר לְחֹשֶׁךְ, בֵּין יִשְׂרָאֵל לָעַמִּים, בֵּין יוֹם הַשְּׁבִיעִי לְשֵׁשֶׁת יְמֵי הַמַּעֲשֶׂה. בֵּין קְדֻשַּׁת שַׁבָּת לִקְדֻשַּׁת יוֹם טוֹב הִבְדַּלְתָּ. וְאֶת־יוֹם הַשְּׁבִיעִי מִשֵּׁשֶׁת יְמֵי הַמַּעֲשֶׂה קִדַּשְׁתָּ. הִבְדַּלְתָּ וְקִדַּשְׁתָּ אֶת־עַמְּךָ יִשְׂרָאֵל בִּקְדֻשָּׁתֶךָ. בָּרוּךְ אַתָּה יְיָ, הַמַּבְדִּיל בֵּין קֹדֶשׁ לְקֹדֶשׁ:

---

who shares that obligation, but not by one who has a lesser obligation or none at all. Thus, in general, everyone can fulfill their obligation to say *Kiddush* by listening to one person say it. But what if that person had already said *Kiddush* and therefore no longer shares an obligation with the others? Under the principle of *arevut* (mu-tual responsibility) that person retains a status as one under the obligation simply by virtue of the fact that the others have not yet discharged theirs. R. Akiva Eiger (*Responsum 7*) rules that there is no dis-tinction at all between men and women regarding *arevut*.

Rabbi Eiger was the son of Moshe and

On other nights begin here:

With your permission!
Blessed are You, Lord, our God, King of the universe, who creates the fruit of the vine.

On Shabbat, add the words in brackets:

Blessed are You, Lord, our God, King of the universe, who has chosen us from among all people, and raised us above all tongues, and made us holy through His commandments. And You, Lord, our God, have given us in love [Sabbaths for rest and] festivals for happiness, feasts and festive seasons for rejoicing [this Sabbath-day and] the day of this Feast of Matzot and this Festival of holy convocation, the Time of our Freedom [in love], a holy convocation, commemorating the departure from Egypt. For You have chosen us and sanctified us from all the nations, and You have given us as a heritage [Shabbat and] Your sacred holidays [in love and favor], in happiness and joy. Blessed are You, Lord, who sanctifies [the Shabbat and] Israel and the festive seasons.

On Saturday night add the following two blessings:

Blessed are You, Lord, our God, King of the universe, Creator of the light of fire.

Blessed are You, Lord, our God, King of the universe, who makes a distinction between sacred and profane, between light and darkness, between Israel and the nations, between the seventh day and the six work-days. You have made a distinction between the holiness of the Shabbat and the holiness of the festival, and You have sanctified the seventh day above the six work-days. You have set apart and made holy Your people Israel with Your holiness. Blessed are You, God, who makes a distinction between holy and holy.

Gittel Guens, but he and his children were known publicly by his mother's maiden name. Her father was Rabbi Akiva Eiger, rav of Pressburg in his day.

The time of our freedom

Slaves have no appreciation of time; they live only in the present. But when we became free, we immediately began to experience time, to be able to recapture the past and plan for the future. For this reason Passover is called *Zeman Herutainu*. It was not only the time of our freedom, but its freedom gave us an appreciation of time

בכל לילה מסיימים:

בָּרוּךְ אַתָּה יְיָ, אֱלֹהֵינוּ מֶלֶךְ הָעוֹלָם, שֶׁהֶחֱיָנוּ וְקִיְּמָנוּ וְהִגִּיעָנוּ לַזְּמַן הַזֶּה:

שׁוֹתִים הַכּוֹס בַּהֲסִיבַת שְׂמֹאל.

וּרְחַץ

נוֹטְלִים יָדַיִם בְּלִי בְּרָכָה.

כַּרְפַּס

לוֹקְחִים כַּרְפַּס (פָּחוֹת מִכַּזַּיִת) וּמַטְבִּילִים אוֹתוֹ בְּמֵי מֶלַח אוֹ בְּחֹמֶץ. וּמְכַוְּנִים בַּבְּרָכָה זוֹ לִפְטֹר גַּם אֶת הַמָּרוֹר, וְאוֹכְלִים בְּלֹא הֲסִיבָה, וְיֵשׁ נוֹהֲגִים לְהָסֵב.

בָּרוּךְ אַתָּה יְיָ, אֱלֹהֵינוּ מֶלֶךְ הָעוֹלָם, בּוֹרֵא פְּרִי הָאֲדָמָה:

יַחַץ

בּוֹצְעִים אֶת הַמַּצָּה הָאֶמְצָעִית לִשְׁנֵי חֲלָקִים לֹא שָׁוִים, אֶת הַפְּרוּסָה הַקְּטַנָּה מַנִּיחִים בֵּין שְׁתֵּי הַמַּצּוֹת הַשְּׁלֵמוֹת, וְאֶת הַפְּרוּסָה הַגְּדוֹלָה מַצְנִיעִים לַאֲפִיקוֹמָן.

(Marisa Savitsky, *Yeshivat Ramaz Likrat Shabbat Haggadah*).

Sheheheyanu at Kiddush

If a woman who said *Sheheheyanu* at candle lighting time says *Kiddush* herself, she should not repeat the blessing. Some authorities hold that she should not even answer *amen* to the *Sheheheyanu* blessing said by another person during *Kiddush*, as it would constitute a *hefsek* (unnecessary interruption); others allow it because the blessing also applies to the other mitzvot of the *seder*. These issues are averted by deferring the saying of *Sheheheyanu* to *Kiddush*.

Yaknehaz

Yaknehaz is the mnemonic acronym used to recall the order of the blessings in the *kiddush* on Saturday night: *Yayin* (the blessing over wine); *Kiddush*; *Ner* (the candle required for the *havdala* ceremony marking the end of Shabbat); *Havdala*; and *Zman* (the *Sheheheyanu* blessing). The German *Jagen-has* (hare hunt) sounds close to it, and medieval Ashkenazic haggadot would therefore sometimes include a scene of a hunter and his hounds.

Yahatz

On a personal level, when we split, the real

12

On all nights, conclude with the following blessing:

Blessed are You, Lord, our God, King of the universe, who has granted us life, sustained us, and enabled us to reach this occasion.

Drink the wine while reclining on the left.

UREHATZ

Hands are washed without reciting the blessing.

KARPAS

Take less than a kezayit (the volume of one olive) of the karpas, dip it into salt-water or vinegar, and recite the following blessing, keeping in mind that it is also for the bitter herbs (of maror and korekh), to be eaten later on:

Blessed are You, Lord, our God, King of the universe, who creates the fruit of the earth.

YAHATZ

Take the middle matzah and break it into two, one piece larger than the other. The larger piece is set aside to serve as afikoman. The smaller piece is put back between the two matzot.

---

challenge is to come back together. When one holds a half, the other approaches with the other half. Part of this matzah becomes the *afikoman* which some of us hide and some of us find. If we have finally found each other, let us not hide again from each other (Beverly Gribitz, *Yeshivat Ramaz Likrat Shabbat Haggadah*).

In the Syrian-Sephardic community, the head of the household holds the napkin containing the matzah in his right hand, puts it over his shoulder and says:

"*Mishaartam*...their remaining possessions tied up in their bags on their shoulders; the children of Israel did as Moses commanded" (*Exodus* 12:34).

The family then asks him: "*Minwen jaiyeh?* (Where are you coming from?)"

He replies: "*Mimitzrayim* (From Egypt)."

They then ask: "*Lawen rayekh?* (Where are you going?)"

He replies: "*Leyerushalayim* (To Jerusalem)."

במנהג ספרד, יש כורכים את החלק הגדול של המצה
במטפחת, מניחים על הכתף ואומרים:

מִשְׁאֲרֹתָם צְרֻרֹת בְּשִׂמְלֹתָם עַל שִׁכְמָם. וּבְנֵי יִשְׂרָאֵל עָשׂוּ
כִּדְבַר מֹשֶׁה.

מַגִּיד

מגלים את המצות ומגביהים את הקערה ואומרים ההגדה.

בנוסחת הרמב"ם, מתחילים כאן:

בְּבָהִלוּ יָצָאנוּ מִמִּצְרַיִם

הָא לַחְמָא עַנְיָא, דִּי אֲכָלוּ אֲבָהֲתָנָא בְּאַרְעָא דְמִצְרָיִם. כָּל דִּכְפִין
יֵיתֵי וְיֵיכֹל, כָּל דִּצְרִיךְ יֵיתֵי וְיִפְסַח. הָשַׁתָּא הָכָא, לְשָׁנָה הַבָּאָה
בְּאַרְעָא דְיִשְׂרָאֵל. הָשַׁתָּא עַבְדֵי, לְשָׁנָה הַבָּאָה בְּנֵי חוֹרִין:

They ask: "Ishu zawatk? (What are your provisions?)"

He replies: "Matzah umaror (Matzah and bitter herbs)."

He then hands the napkin to the next oldest who repeats the whole process. This continues in turn until all present have participated.

Shulhan Arukh (*Orah Hayim* 483:6) says that one puts the broken matzah that is set aside for the *afikoman* in a napkin and gives it to another (one might suspect for safekeeping from the children who would attempt to steal it!). R. Yair Bakhrakh (*Mekor Hayim* commentary on *Shulhan Arukh*, ibid.) quotes the custom of putting the napkin on one's shoulder and then walking to and fro, noting one comment that this was the custom in Germany and another that "he had never seen anyone who did it." However, variations on this custom are widespread in many Sephardic communities.

R. Yair Bakhrakh is more widely known for his book of responsa, *Havvot Yair*, "the villages of Yair." He took for his title a phrase from the Bible (*Numbers* 31:42, *Deut.* 3:14) that contained his name but, as he explains in his introduction, he also took the name to memorialize his grandmother Havva, whom he describes as "exceptional in her generation in Torah." She was the granddaughter of the Maharal of Prague, and her mother had assured her a solid education in Bible, Talmud, Midrash and responsa. She would sometimes take issue with rabbinical authorities, R. Yair writes, and she was recognized as correct; he himself quotes her opinion in his writing. "I have named the book *Havvot Yair*: Yair, a descendant of the pious women Havva."

In contemporary discussions, R. Bakhrakh is often cited for his responsum (*Havvot Yair* 222) forbidding bereaved daughters to say Kaddish. He conceded in his responsum that the daughter's Kaddish

*In the Sephardic custom, some wrap the larger piece of matzah
in a napkin, put it over their shoulder and say:*

Their remaining possessions tied up in their bags on their shoulders,
the children of Israel did as Moses commanded.

MAGID

The matzot are uncovered and the seder plate raised.

Rambam adds:

We left Egypt hurriedly.

This is the bread of affliction that our fathers ate in the land of Egypt.
Let all who are hungry come and eat; let whoever is in need come
and conduct the Seder of Passover. This year we are here, next year in
the land of Israel. This year [we are] slaves; next year we will be free
people.

---

brings *nahat ruah* (peace) to the deceased, that women participate in the *mitzvah* of *kiddush haShem* and that Kaddish could be said because a *minyan* of men was present. But in the final analysis he would not allow her to say Kaddish as he feared that such an innovation might weaken allegiance to existing Jewish customs. Such strategies are not always effective when transferred to a contemporary society three hundred years later. Thus, R. Aaron Soloveitchik rules: "Nowadays, when there are Jews fighting for equality for men and women in matters such as *aliyot*, if Orthodox rabbis prevent women from saying Kaddish when there is a possibility for allowing it, it will strengthen the influence of Reform and Conservative rabbis. It is therefore forbidden to prevent daughters from saying Kaddish" (*Od Yisrael Yosef Beni Hai*, no. 32).

Let all who are hungry come and eat
Yaffa Eliach relates that when Rebbetzin

Bronia Spira was in the Bergen Belsen concentration camp with her two small sons Zvi and Yitzhak, she spared no effort to continue to educate them in the spirit of Torah. When Passover approached, she insisted that the children learn all the laws and customs of the holiday. She mannaged to obtain some beets and potatoes so that they would be able to manage without bread, and even arranged to sell her *hametz* to a non-Jew, a gentile woman from Prague who was married to a Jewish lawyer and who was also in Bergen-Belsen with her. When others taunted her about such concerns, she replied, "I learned the Jewish tradition in my father's home when I was a child. Now it is my duty as a Jewish mother to teach it to my children in my home."

When Passover ended, a woman came running to Bronia. "The Rabbi of Pruchnik is almost dead," she said. "He hardly ate during the holiday and now refuses to eat *hametz* that has not been sold prior to

מניחים את הקערה ומסלקים לקצה השולחן. מוזגים כוס שני, וכאן שואלים:

מַה נִּשְׁתַּנָּה הַלַּיְלָה הַזֶּה מִכָּל הַלֵּילוֹת?

נוסח ספרד:	נוסח אשכנז:
שֶׁבְּכָל הַלֵּילוֹת אֵין אָנוּ מַטְבִּילִין אֲפִלּוּ פַּעַם אֶחָת, הַלַּיְלָה הַזֶּה שְׁתֵּי פְעָמִים:	שֶׁבְּכָל הַלֵּילוֹת אָנוּ אוֹכְלִין חָמֵץ וּמַצָּה, הַלַּיְלָה הַזֶּה כֻּלּוֹ מַצָּה:
שֶׁבְּכָל הַלֵּילוֹת אָנוּ אוֹכְלִין חָמֵץ וּמַצָּה, הַלַּיְלָה הַזֶּה כֻּלּוֹ מַצָּה:	שֶׁבְּכָל הַלֵּילוֹת אָנוּ אוֹכְלִין שְׁאָר יְרָקוֹת, הַלַּיְלָה הַזֶּה מָרוֹר:
שֶׁבְּכָל הַלֵּילוֹת אָנוּ אוֹכְלִין שְׁאָר יְרָקוֹת הַלַּיְלָה הַזֶּה מָרוֹר:	שֶׁבְּכָל הַלֵּילוֹת אֵין אָנוּ מַטְבִּילִין אֲפִלּוּ פַּעַם אֶחָת, הַלַּיְלָה הַזֶּה שְׁתֵּי פְעָמִים:
שֶׁבְּכָל הַלֵּילוֹת אָנוּ אוֹכְלִין בֵּין יוֹשְׁבִין וּבֵין מְסֻבִּין, הַלַּיְלָה הַזֶּה כֻּלָּנוּ מְסֻבִּין:	שֶׁבְּכָל הַלֵּילוֹת אָנוּ אוֹכְלִין בֵּין יוֹשְׁבִין וּבֵין מְסֻבִּין, הַלַּיְלָה הַזֶּה כֻּלָּנוּ מְסֻבִּין:

---

the holiday. I heard that you are the only person in the camp who sold your *hametz*." Bronia did not hesitate and took a loaf of white bread, her most precious possession, and gave it for the Rabbi. People around her asked how she could give her children's bread away. "What I learned and saw at my father's home, I want my children to see and learn in my home," she responded. "I could not choose the home but I can preserve the spirit."

When her son Zvi asked where they would be next Passover, she responded, "In Jerusalem." When he asked how she knew,

she replied, "I learned it in my father's house" (*Hasidic Tales of the Holocaust*).

Ma Nishtanah

Nechama Leibowitz points out that the structure of these questions is that of a *kushiyah* as opposed to a *she'ela*, which is a simple informational question. A *kushiyah* takes note of something that deviates from the norm, reflecting a contrast or seeming contradiction to what we know and would expect based on our previous knowledge or experience. The *kushiyah* is the fundamental pedagogic instrument of

The seder plate is moved aside, the second cup is poured, and the questions asked:

Mah Nishtanah, What makes this night different from all other nights?

Ashkenazic custom:	Sephardic custom:
On all nights we eat *hametz* or matzah, and on this night only matzah!	On all nights we need not dip even once, on this night we do so twice!
On all nights we eat any kind of vegetables, and on this night maror!	On all nights we eat *hametz* or matzah, and on this night only matzah!
On all nights we need not dip even once, on this night we do so twice!	On all nights we eat any kind of vegetables, and on this night maror!
On all nights we eat sitting upright or reclining, and on this night we all recline!	On all nights we eat sitting upright or reclining, and on this night we all recline!

---

both the Pesah Seder and biblical exegesis (*Studies in the Haggadah from the Teachings of Nechama Leibowitz*).

The Ashkenazic custom is to ask about Torah obligations first (matzah and maror) and then about the rabbinic obligations (dipping and reclining). The Sephardic custom follows the order of the *seder*. The Mishnah (*Pesahim* 10:4) has no question about reclining; instead it asks, "Each night we eat boiled or roasted meat, but tonight only roasted."

According to the Mishnah, these questions were not asked originally by the child. Rather, "The second cup is poured and here the child asks." The question is not an obligation, but a consequence of curiosity having been piqued by the change in the regular order of things. If, however, the child does not have the wherewithal to notice these changes, the leader asks, "Why

is this night different from all other nights?" and proceeds to offer four examples.

Secular kibbutzim in Israel have a "nontheistic" *seder* celebrating the national liberation from Egypt. Their haggadah has the question, "On all nights the adults eat in the main dining room of the kibbutz and the children eat in the children's dining room. Tonight we all eat together."

We all recline

The original Talmudic ruling was that "a woman who is in the presence of her husband does not recline, but if she is an important woman, she must recline" (TB *Pesahim* 108a). Rashbam there explains that she may not recline because "the fear of her husband is upon her as she is subjugated to him." The Mordehai (*Pesahim* 108a) rules that "all our women are important and must recline," a position endorsed and codi-

מחזירים את הקערה למקומה:

עֲבָדִים הָיִינוּ לְפַרְעֹה בְּמִצְרָיִם. וַיּוֹצִיאֵנוּ יְיָ אֱלֹהֵינוּ מִשָּׁם, בְּיָד חֲזָקָה וּבִזְרוֹעַ נְטוּיָה. וְאִלּוּ לֹא הוֹצִיא הַקָּדוֹשׁ בָּרוּךְ הוּא אֶת־אֲבוֹתֵינוּ מִמִּצְרַיִם, הֲרֵי אָנוּ וּבָנֵינוּ וּבְנֵי בָנֵינוּ, מְשֻׁעְבָּדִים הָיִינוּ לְפַרְעֹה בְּמִצְרָיִם. וַאֲפִלּוּ כֻּלָּנוּ חֲכָמִים, כֻּלָּנוּ נְבוֹנִים, כֻּלָּנוּ זְקֵנִים, כֻּלָּנוּ יוֹדְעִים אֶת־הַתּוֹרָה מִצְוָה עָלֵינוּ לְסַפֵּר בִּיצִיאַת מִצְרָיִם. וְכָל הַמַּרְבֶּה לְסַפֵּר בִּיצִיאַת מִצְרַיִם, הֲרֵי זֶה מְשֻׁבָּח:

fied by Ramo (*Shulhan Arukh Orah Hayim* 472:4). Such a ruling cannot be read as describing the individual reality in each and every household. Rather, it prescribes a general *Anschauung* with respect to the status of women. Thus, Rabbi Haim David HaLevi, the late Chief Rabbi of Tel Aviv, rules that "the rationale for the position that 'a woman who is in the presence of her husband does not recline' has expired, and therefore the halakhah should be changed. Perhaps at different times or places the fear of a woman's husband was upon her and she was subjugated to him. However, this is not true nowadays, as no woman is subjugated to her husband and the fear of him is not upon her. She therefore must recline" (*Mayim Hayim*, 1:128). Once it was established that "all our women are important," an individual wife and her husband have lost the option of her not reclining so that she may serve the meal. "She must recline."

Some Ashkenazic commentators maintain that, inasmuch as it is not the current custom in general society for prominent women to recline while eating, women at the *seder* may still not be obligated to do so, as the original goal was only to mimic the behavior of rich people at their regular meals. But no one is of the opinion that the

original principle is operative or that we should adopt the position that women in general are not important. All women in our community are important.

We were slaves
Though we may not be in a state of slavery now, the past is something that we must carry with us wherever our future leads us. And herein lies the similarity between the movement from sin to repentance, on the one hand, and from *galut* to *ge'ulah*, on the other. Repentance is not about negating the memory of who we used to be or becoming a newborn person with no past. Just as the experience of having been slaves in Egypt must inform who we are today, so too who we were yesterday must inform who we are today, even if we have grown in new ways. Since sinning cuts to the core of our personality, we cannot surgically remove the sin without removing other parts of our identity as well. Repentance is about using our past to transform the future, never losing sight of that past, however painful it may be. Similarly, we cannot reach a state of personal or national redemption without preserving the memory of what it was to be enslaved. Change, or psychological redemption, is a difficult process, one with which the gen-

*The tray is restored to its place and the matzah uncovered
during the recitation of the Haggadah.*

We were slaves to Pharaoh in Egypt, and the Lord, our God, took us out from there with a strong hand and with an outstretched arm. If the Holy One, blessed be He, had not taken our fathers out of Egypt, then we, our children and our children's children would have remained enslaved to Pharaoh in Egypt. Even if all of us were wise, all of us understanding, all of us knowing the Torah, it is a *mitzvah* to tell the story of the exodus from Egypt; and everyone who discusses the exodus from Egypt at length is praiseworthy.

---

eration that wandered through the desert struggled for forty years after they were physically redeemed. The redemption was not felt in a day (Jennie Rosenfeld, *Vehigadet Levitekh*, JOFA).

It is a mitzvah to tell the story of the Exodus

There is widespread agreement that both men and women are obligated to tell *sippur yitziat Mitzrayim*, the story of the Exodus, at the *seder*; there is, however, a difference of opinion as to whether women have a biblical obligation as do the men, or if their obligation is only rabbinic. The main consequence of the debate is whether men may fulfill their obligation through a woman's conducting the entire *seder* or even a part of it. One may fulfill one's obligation by listening to another fulfilling his or her obligation only if the person actually performing the mitzvah has the same or greater obligation as do those who are listening.

The general principle arguing for women's biblical exemption from this mitzvah is that it is meant to be fulfilled at a specific time (at the *seder*), and as a rule women are exempt from positive time-bound commandments, even though they are fully obligated in all prohibitions that are in effect only at specific times. The main exception

to this rule is that when time-bound obligations are tied up with the prohibitions, women are obligated in both. Thus women are obligated in *Kiddush* and all other positive obligations on Shabbat even though they are time bound because in the two versions of the Decalogue *"Zakhor"* (which represents the positive obligations) and *"Shamor"* (which represents the negative prohibitions) were said in the same utterance. Whoever is obligated in the prohibitions of *Shamor* is likewise obligated in the commandments of *Zakhor*.

Rabbi Yehoshua ben Levi said, "Women are obligated to drink the four cups [of wine at the *seder*], as they were involved in the miracle" (BT *Pesahim* 108a–b). Rashbam and Tosafot interpret this to mean that it was because of the merits of the righteous women of that generation that they were saved. However, the principle that "they too were involved in the miracle" is generally invoked to obligate women in rabbinic mitzvot, leaving the possibility that women are obligated in the mitzvah of *sippur yitziat Mitzrayim* on only a rabbinic level. Rabbeinu Yosef Ish Yerushalim (TB *Megilla* 4a, *Tosafot s.v., she-af hein*) contends that this reason is invoked here only to preclude the assumption that just as women are exempt from the mitzvah of sitting in

מַעֲשֶׂה בְּרַבִּי אֱלִיעֶזֶר וְרַבִּי יְהוֹשֻׁעַ וְרַבִּי אֶלְעָזָר בֶּן־עֲזַרְיָה וְרַבִּי עֲקִיבָא וְרַבִּי טַרְפוֹן, שֶׁהָיוּ מְסֻבִּין בִּבְנֵי־בְרַק, וְהָיוּ מְסַפְּרִים בִּיצִיאַת מִצְרַיִם כָּל־אוֹתוֹ הַלַּיְלָה, עַד שֶׁבָּאוּ תַלְמִידֵיהֶם וְאָמְרוּ לָהֶם: רַבּוֹתֵינוּ, הִגִּיעַ זְמַן קְרִיאַת שְׁמַע שֶׁל שַׁחֲרִית:

אָמַר רַבִּי אֶלְעָזָר בֶּן־עֲזַרְיָה: הֲרֵי אֲנִי כְּבֶן שִׁבְעִים שָׁנָה, וְלֹא זָכִיתִי שֶׁתֵּאָמֵר יְצִיאַת מִצְרַיִם בַּלֵּילוֹת, עַד שֶׁדְּרָשָׁהּ בֶּן־זוֹמָא. שֶׁנֶּאֱמַר: לְמַעַן תִּזְכֹּר אֶת יוֹם צֵאתְךָ מֵאֶרֶץ מִצְרַיִם כֹּל יְמֵי חַיֶּיךָ. יְמֵי חַיֶּיךָ הַיָּמִים. כֹּל יְמֵי חַיֶּיךָ, הַלֵּילוֹת. וַחֲכָמִים אוֹמְרִים: יְמֵי חַיֶּיךָ, הָעוֹלָם הַזֶּה. כֹּל יְמֵי חַיֶּיךָ, לְהָבִיא לִימוֹת הַמָּשִׁיחַ:

בָּרוּךְ הַמָּקוֹם, בָּרוּךְ הוּא. בָּרוּךְ שֶׁנָּתַן תּוֹרָה לְעַמּוֹ יִשְׂרָאֵל, בָּרוּךְ הוּא. כְּנֶגֶד אַרְבָּעָה בָנִים דִּבְּרָה תוֹרָה: אֶחָד חָכָם, וְאֶחָד רָשָׁע, וְאֶחָד תָּם, וְאֶחָד שֶׁאֵינוֹ יוֹדֵעַ לִשְׁאוֹל:

---

the *sukkah*, they might be exempt from the mitzvah of *sippur yitziat Mitzrayim*. They are indeed obligated from the Torah in this mitzvah.

Rambam (Maimonides) explicitly writes (*Sefer Hamitzvot, Positive Mitzvot* 248) that women are obligated in the biblical obligation of *sippur yitziat Mitzrayim*, a position repeated by the *Hinukh* (*Commandment* 21). Rav Yosef Shalom Elyashiv explains that the mitzvah of *sippur yitziat Mitzrayim* was given in Egypt before *matan Torah* at Sinai, at which time the exemption of time-bound commandments was initiated. Women therefore remain obligated in the mitzvah (*Haseder Ha'arukh* I:61:2(6)).

Rabbi Akiva and Rabbi Tarfon

Akiva was a shepherd. When the daughter of his employer saw how pious and capable he was, she told him, If I become secretly betrothed to you, would you go off to the house of study? He agreed, and she sent him away. After twelve years, he returned with twelve thousand disciples. At the time, he heard an old man admonish his wife, How long will you live the life of a living widow? On hearing her reply, "If he listened to me, he would stay away another twelve years," he left again and stayed in the House of Study another twelve years, returning eventually with twenty-four thousand disciples. "What is mine and yours is hers," he told them, recognizing the debt all owe to her values, vision and determination (*TB Ketubot* 62a).

One day R. Tarfon's mother's sandals split and broke, and as she could not mend them, she had to walk across the courtyard barefoot. So R. Tarfon kept stretching his hands under her feet, so that she might walk over them all the way. One day he

It happened that Rabbi Eliezer, Rabbi Yehoshua, Rabbi Eleazar ben Azaryah, Rabbi Akiva and Rabbi Tarphon were reclining [at a seder] in B'nei Berak. They were discussing the exodus from Egypt all that night, until their students came and told them: "Our Masters! The time has come for reciting the morning *Shema!*"

Rabbi Eleazar ben Azaryah said: "I am like a man seventy years old, yet I did not succeed in proving that the exodus from Egypt must be mentioned at night, until Ben Zoma explained it: "It is said, 'That you may remember the day you left Egypt all the days of your life;' now 'the days of your life' refers to the days, [and the additional word] 'all' indicates the inclusion of the nights!" The sages, however, said: "'The days of your life' refers to the present-day world; and 'all' indicates the inclusion of the days of Mashiah."

Blessed is the Omnipresent One, blessed be He! Blessed is He who gave the Torah to His people Israel, blessed be He! The Torah speaks of four children: One is wise, one is wicked, one is simple and one does not know how to ask.

---

was ill, and the Rabbis came to visit him. His mother said to them, "Pray for my son Tarfon, for he honors me more than is my due." "What has he done for you?" they asked. She told them what had happened. They replied, "If he had done to you a thousand times more, he would not have done half of the honor required in the Law" (*TJ Kiddushin* 1).

The four children

The Haggadah speaks *"keneged arba banim"* instead of *"al arba banim,"* seeming to imply that there is an element of confrontation (*neged*) in the exchange. But the root of *keneged* – n.g.d. – is the same as that of *haggadah* and *veheggadeta*, which has the meaning of drawing someone to listen. The four types of children must be taught in their own special way and according to their own special needs (*Dina Haramati*).

"Banim" in Hebrew can mean "sons" or "children," and the Talmud draws halakhic conclusions depending on the case. Here the translation is clearly "children." The obligation to teach the story of the Exodus and its implications as a basis of our faith applies to sons and daughters alike (*Haggadat Hazon Ovadiah* 21).

It is not surprising that a discussion of the four children appears at the *seder*. After all, the family dinner is a primary instrument of human education, one of the important places at which family values are articulated and transmitted. Here too the question of responding to different children in different ways must be explored.

How, indeed, could one family have both a wise and wicked child? Rabbi Shimshon Rafael Hirsch explains how Isaac and Rebecca had such different children, a Jacob and an Esav, emerge from the same To-

Ariana Nehmad

חָכָם מַה הוּא אוֹמֵר? מָה הָעֵדֹת וְהַחֻקִּים וְהַמִּשְׁפָּטִים, אֲשֶׁר צִוָּה יְיָ אֱלֹהֵינוּ אֶתְכֶם? וְאַף אַתָּה אֱמָר־לוֹ כְּהִלְכוֹת הַפֶּסַח: אֵין מַפְטִירִין אַחַר הַפֶּסַח אֲפִיקוֹמָן:

רָשָׁע מַה הוּא אוֹמֵר? מָה הָעֲבֹדָה הַזֹּאת לָכֶם? לָכֶם וְלֹא לוֹ. וּלְפִי שֶׁהוֹצִיא אֶת־עַצְמוֹ מִן הַכְּלָל, כָּפַר בָּעִקָּר. וְאַף אַתָּה הַקְהֵה אֶת־שִׁנָּיו, וֶאֱמָר־לוֹ: בַּעֲבוּר זֶה, עָשָׂה יְיָ לִי, בְּצֵאתִי מִמִּצְרָיִם, לִי וְלֹא־לוֹ. אִלּוּ הָיָה שָׁם, לֹא הָיָה נִגְאָל:

---

rah household: "To try to bring up a Jacob and an Esav in the same college, make them have the same habits and hobbies, want to teach and educate them in the same way for some studious, sedate, meditative life is the surest way to court disaster.... Had Isaac and Rebecca studied Esav's nature and character early enough and asked themselves how can even an Esav...be won over to the service of God,...who can say what a different aspect of the whole history of the ages might have been presented" (Commentary to *Genesis* 25:27).

Treating every child the same is not the only way to court educational disaster; letting stereotypes decide arbitrary differences in educational goals is another. Despite statistical difference in interests, we no longer think that women should necessarily learn literature while men should engage in science and math. Yet somehow many feel that women should necessarily restrict their studies to Bible and its commentaries while men should study Talmud and *poskim*.

The Wise Woman

Hakhamah refers to a professional midwife (*Rashi*, TB *Shabbat 128b and Meiri*). Eli-sheva Baumgarten notes that in the Middle Ages the midwife was an expert in not only birthing but other gynecological problems – and an *Ishah Hakhamah* was even able to offer competent medical advice to a *mohel* who had made a surgical error during a circumcision (*Zion* LXV:1). Harry Friedenwald quotes the license granted in 1419 by Archbishop John II of Würzburg allowing "Sarah the Jewess, the doctoress" the right to practice medicine throughout the bishopric: "Thus we shall let it stand for the time thus agreed upon for the next three years so that she may practice her profession without interference on our part or of those belonging to us, unconditionally, and should anyone intend to prosecute her or actually do so, against such one we shall take action to the best of our ability so that he be stopped unconditionally." Not all fared so well. Towards the end of the fifteenth century, the Jews of Trent were martyred as a result of the denunciations of Bernardinus of Siena. At the blood libel trial of the Jews for the alleged murder of the child Simon of Trent, the Jewish woman physician Brunetta was charged with having furnished the needles used to draw the blood (*The Jews and Medicine*).

The wise one, what does he say? "What are the testimonies, the statutes and the laws which the Lord, our God, has commanded you?" You, in turn, shall instruct him in the laws of Passover, [up to] "one is not to eat any dessert after the Passover-lamb."

The wicked one, what does he say? "What is this service to you?!" He says "to you," but not to him! By thus excluding himself from the community he has denied that which is fundamental. You should therefore blunt his teeth and say to him: "It is because of this that the Lord did for me when I left Egypt"; "for me" – but not for him! If he had been there, he would not have been redeemed!

Ishah Hakhamah also refers to the wife or daughter of a *talmid hakham* (*Rashi*, *TB Shabbat* 95a). Rav Nahman would stand up in honor of the wife of Rav Huna, as the wife of a *talmid hakham* must be shown the same respect as that shown the sage himself (*TB Shavuot* 30b). Rabbi Ovadiah Yosef points out that such respect must be shown to a women who herself is a Torah scholar, even though women do not have the same halakhic obligation to pursue abstract halakhic studies as do men (*Yehave Da'at* 3:72). Presumably, the same respect would have to be shown her husband, even if he himself were not a *talmid hakham*.

The Wicked Child

The wicked child does not ask simply "What is this *avoda*?" but rather "What is this to *you*?" The question is designed to hurt, and the parent responds with anger in retaliation: You have excluded yourself from the community and from participation in our celebration. But why, asks Avivah Gottlieb Zornberg, should this exclusion trouble the questioner who has already excluded himself?

"Eating a meal with others, however, is an experience that, in a primary way, is a ful-fillment of desire. Not merely the sensual aspects of the meal – the smell, the sounds, the sights, the textures, the tastes – but also the sense of community felt by those who eat together – they constitute a moment from which it is hard to be excluded. So-cially and culturally, the questioner is made to feel his 'outside-ness' as an untenable attitude. The cost of the question is borne in upon him, making him aware that a facile 'outside-ness' is an illusion. He discovers his desire to participate, to be part of the story. There is, in fact, no answer to the alienated violence of his question" (*The Particulars of Rapture*).

Though the *Rasha*'s question reveals his nature, he has nevertheless made the effort to attend the seder and to take part in the discussion. The reply "*Hak-heh et shinav*" therefore seems overly harsh. But perhaps the reply can be translated as, "Sharpen and improve his *shin* letters." There are two forms of the letter *shin* – the three-branched *shin* and the four-branched one – that appear on the two sides of the head *tefillin* worn every weekday morning. These letters represent the connection to one's roots: the three-branched *shin* represents the connection to the three forefathers – Abraham,

תָּם מַה הוּא אוֹמֵר? מַה זֹּאת? וְאָמַרְתָּ אֵלָיו: בְּחֹזֶק יָד הוֹצִיאָנוּ יְיָ מִמִּצְרַיִם מִבֵּית עֲבָדִים:

וְשֶׁאֵינוֹ יוֹדֵעַ לִשְׁאוֹל, אַתְּ פְּתַח לוֹ. שֶׁנֶּאֱמַר: וְהִגַּדְתָּ לְבִנְךָ, בַּיּוֹם הַהוּא לֵאמֹר: בַּעֲבוּר זֶה עָשָׂה יְיָ לִי, בְּצֵאתִי מִמִּצְרַיִם:

יָכוֹל מֵרֹאשׁ חֹדֶשׁ, תַּלְמוּד לוֹמַר: בַּיּוֹם הַהוּא. אִי בַּיּוֹם הַהוּא, יָכוֹל מִבְּעוֹד יוֹם, תַּלְמוּד לוֹמַר: בַּעֲבוּר זֶה. בַּעֲבוּר זֶה לֹא אָמַרְתִּי, אֶלָּא בְּשָׁעָה שֶׁיֵּשׁ מַצָּה וּמָרוֹר מֻנָּחִים לְפָנֶיךָ:

מִתְּחִלָּה עוֹבְדֵי עֲבוֹדָה זָרָה הָיוּ אֲבוֹתֵינוּ, וְעַכְשָׁו קֵרְבָנוּ הַמָּקוֹם

Isaac and Jacob – while the less well-known four-branched *shin* symbolizes the connection to the four mothers – Sarah, Rebecca, Rachel and Leah. The two outer letters of *rasha* – the *reish* and *ayin* – form the word *ra*, evil. We turn to the *Rasha* and say: You are not evil, for at your core your *shins* are still intact; your connection to your roots and to your past is evident from your presence and participation. Is it not time to sharpen and strengthen this connection? (Levia Cooper)

The idiom "*Hakheh et shinav,* you in turn should set his teeth on edge" is derived from the parable with which *B'nei Yisrael* mistakenly excused its sins: "The fathers ate unripe grapes and the children's teeth will be set on edge" (*Ezekial* 18:2) – i.e., our children will pay for our sins, so let's sin on. This statement betrays a stunning disregard both for the fate of the next generation and for the will of Hashem. How fitting an admonishment for the wicked child, whose statement excludes himself from his parents' people and denies the principles of our faith in Hashem. The child's teeth should be set on edge, to defend the continuity of the Jewish people and affirm the will of Hashem, because this child has brought this very punishment upon himself (Laurie Novick).

Rosh Hodesh
Rosh Hodesh is a special holiday for women on which they generally should not do any work (*Shulhan Arukh Orah Hayim* 417:1). When the people demanded of Aaron that he make a god for them, he told them "Take off the gold rings that are on the ears of your wives, your sons, and your daughters, and bring them to me" (*Exodus* 32:2). He reasoned that the women would refuse to take part and the project would fall apart. Indeed, the women refused to give their jewelry, but the men, who at that time also wore earrings in accordance with the Egyptian custom, contributed their own jewelry, as the verse says, "They took off the gold earrings that were in their ears" (*Exodus* 32:3) – their ears, and not their wives.' As a reward, it is the women who observe Rosh Hodesh by refraining from work (*Pirkei*

24

The simple child, what does he say? "What is this?" Thus you shall say to him: "With a strong hand the Lord took us out of Egypt, from the house of slaves."

As for the one who does not know how to ask, you must initiate him, as it is said: "You shall tell your child on that day, 'It is because of this that the Lord did for me when I left Egypt.'"

One may think that [the discussion of the exodus] must be from Rosh Hodesh, the first of the month. The Torah therefore says, "On that day." "On that day," however, could mean while it is yet day-time; the Torah therefore says, "It is because of this." The expression "because of this" can only be used when matzah and maror are placed before you.

In the beginning our ancestors served idols; but now the Omnipresent

---

de-Rabbi Elazar 54). There is no custom for men to refrain from work on Rosh Hodesh (*Mishnah Berurah* 417, n. 2).

Originally, the holidays were instituted in honor of the Patriarchs: Passover in honor of Abraham, who was visited by the three angels on Passover; Rosh Ha-Shannah in honor of Isaac, as the ram's horn sounded at Sinai was from the ram substituted for him at the *Akeida*; Sukkot in honor of Jacob, who made *sukkot* for his cattle (*Genesis* 33:17); and the twelve celebrations of Rosh Hodesh in honor of the founders of the twelve tribes. After the sin of the Golden Calf, the holiday was transferred to the women in honor of their refusing to participate in the sin (*Tur Shulhan Arukh* 417). Another reason for the special status Rosh Hodesh has for women is that they refresh their marriages each month after returning from the *mikve*, just as the moon refreshes itself each Rosh Hodesh (*ibid, Darkhei Moshe*).

The custom to refrain from work does not have the same status as the prohibition of working on Shabbat and holidays. Exactly which work women refrain from doing is a matter of custom. Rabbi Yehiel Epstein writes that in his community housewives refrained from work but professionals did not, as the custom was surely not to create economic loss (*Arukh ha-Shulhan* 417:10). The important thing is that women not treat Rosh Hodesh as a normal work day. If the custom is that women refrain from work on only one of the days of a two-day Rosh Hodesh celebration, it is the second which should be observed (*Mishnah Berurah* 417, n. 4).

In North African Jewish communities, Rosh Hodesh Tevet is observed as "*Rosh Hodesh haBanot*" in commemoration of Yehudit's contribution to the victory celebrated on Hanukka. Women would gather together after candle lighting for a celebration of singing and eating. Yael Levine suggests (*Kolekh*, no. 75) that this observance in honor of a true Jewish heroine should be appropriately adapted and invigorated to include widespread celebration of the

לַעֲבוֹדָתוֹ. שֶׁנֶּאֱמַר: וַיֹּאמֶר יְהוֹשֻׁעַ אֶל־כָּל־הָעָם. כֹּה אָמַר יְיָ אֱלֹהֵי יִשְׂרָאֵל, בְּעֵבֶר הַנָּהָר יָשְׁבוּ אֲבוֹתֵיכֶם מֵעוֹלָם, תֶּרַח אֲבִי אַבְרָהָם וַאֲבִי נָחוֹר, וַיַּעַבְדוּ אֱלֹהִים אֲחֵרִים: וָאֶקַּח אֶת־אֲבִיכֶם אֶת־אַבְרָהָם מֵעֵבֶר הַנָּהָר, וָאוֹלֵךְ אוֹתוֹ בְּכָל־אֶרֶץ כְּנָעַן. וָאַרְבֶּה אֶת־זַרְעוֹ, וָאֶתֶּן לוֹ אֶת־יִצְחָק: וָאֶתֵּן לְיִצְחָק אֶת־יַעֲקֹב וְאֶת־ עֵשָׂו. וָאֶתֵּן לְעֵשָׂו אֶת־הַר שֵׂעִיר, לָרֶשֶׁת אוֹתוֹ. וְיַעֲקֹב וּבָנָיו יָרְדוּ מִצְרָיִם:

בָּרוּךְ שׁוֹמֵר הַבְטָחָתוֹ לְיִשְׂרָאֵל, בָּרוּךְ הוּא. שֶׁהַקָּדוֹשׁ בָּרוּךְ הוּא חִשַּׁב אֶת־הַקֵּץ, לַעֲשׂוֹת כְּמָה שֶׁאָמַר לְאַבְרָהָם אָבִינוּ בִּבְרִית בֵּין הַבְּתָרִים, שֶׁנֶּאֱמַר: וַיֹּאמֶר לְאַבְרָם, יָדֹעַ תֵּדַע כִּי־גֵר יִהְיֶה זַרְעֶךָ בְּאֶרֶץ לֹא לָהֶם וַעֲבָדוּם, וְעִנּוּ אֹתָם אַרְבַּע מֵאוֹת שָׁנָה: וְגַם אֶת־ הַגּוֹי אֲשֶׁר יַעֲבֹדוּ דָּן אָנֹכִי, וְאַחֲרֵי כֵן יֵצְאוּ בִּרְכֻשׁ גָּדוֹל:

---

increased and unprecedented advanced Torah found among contemporary Jewish women.

In the beginning our ancestors served idols

In his commentary to the Haggadah (*Olat Reayah* II, 261) Rav Kook views the fact that the Jewish people emerged out of paganism as a necessary step in our religious development. Were it not for this preparatory ground, the likelihood is that an intense yearning for the holy would have led us to an unhealthy variety of other-worldliness and an over-cerebral spirituality, thereby divorcing us from connection with material affairs and the imagination necessary for *tikkun olam*.

We might add that it was precisely this balance between earthliness and visionary faith idealized by R. Kook that characterizes women's role in the saga of *yetziat*

Mitzrayim. This was first demonstrated in the determination of *benot Yisrael* to seduce their husbands, playfully goading them into intimacy through erotic mirror games, despite Pharaoh's decree to kill all their male offspring (*Midrash Tanhuma Parshat Pekudei*, simman 9; see also *Shemot Rabba* 1:13; *TB Sotah* 11b). The point was reiterated in women's contribution of these same mirrors to the building of the Mishkan. According to the midrash (*Tanhuma, ibid*), Moshe's initial reaction was fury at such sacrilege. God, however, rebuked him, thereby affirming women's understanding that holiness is integrally bound up with this world and the healthy passions of life (Tamar Ross).

I gave him Isaac

"The greatness of the woman," writes Rabbi Joseph B. Soloveitchik, "manifests itself at the hour of crisis, when the situation does

One has brought us close to His service, as it is said: "Joshua said to all the people: Thus said the Lord, the God of Israel, 'Your ancestors used to live on the other side of the river – Terah, the father of Abraham and the father of Nahor, and they served other gods. I took your father Abraham from beyond the river, and I led him throughout the whole land of Canaan. I increased his seed and gave him Isaac, and to Isaac I gave Jacob and Esau. To Esau I gave Mount Seir to possess it, and Jacob and his children went down to Egypt.'"

Blessed is He who keeps His promise to Israel, blessed be He! For the Holy One, blessed be He, calculated the end [of the bondage], in order to do as He had said to our father Abraham at the "Covenant between the Portions," as it is said: "He said to Abraham, 'You shall know that your seed will be strangers in a land that is not theirs, and they will enslave them and make them suffer, for four hundred years. But I shall also judge the nation whom they shall serve, and afterwards they shall leave with great wealth.'"

---

not lend itself to piecemeal understanding but requires instead instantaneous action that flows from the very depths of a sensitive personality. 'God gave woman *binah yeterah*, an additional measure of knowledge over men' (*Niddah* 45b).

"God lays emphasis upon Sarah's role in the realization of the covenantal society. Abraham's offspring are not taken into this esoteric community if their mother happens to be Hagar and not Sarah. Later, when Sarah demands the expulsion of Ishmael and Abraham is not eager to comply with her request, God tells him in terse terms, 'Let it not be grievous in your sight because of the lad, and because of your bondwoman; in all that Sarah has said unto you, hearken unto her voice, for in Isaac shall your seed be called' (*Genesis* 21:12).

"Rebecca is responsible for the covenant being transmitted to Jacob instead of Esau. Isaac had contemplated entrusting the spiritual heritage to his oldest son. At the hour of crisis Rebecca intervened and thereby determined the historical destiny of the covenantal community. She sent Jacob to Haran to marry her nieces" (*Family Redeemed*).

Jacob and his children went down to Egypt

Among those going down to Egypt was Serah bat Asher (*Genesis* 46:17). It was she whom the brothers selected to reveal to Jacob that Joseph was alive in Egypt, and she cleverly did so in a poetic way that avoided his suffering the shock (*Midrash HaGadol* 45:26). Having restored life to Jacob, she is blessed with never having tasted death and entered Paradise alive (*Torah Shelemah* on Gen. 45:26). She is the authority who convinces the elders that Moses is the promised redeemer (*Pirkei deRabbi*

מכסים את המצות ומגביהים את הכוס ואומרים:

וְהִיא שֶׁעָמְדָה לַאֲבוֹתֵינוּ וְלָנוּ. שֶׁלֹּא אֶחָד בִּלְבָד, עָמַד עָלֵינוּ לְכַלּוֹתֵנוּ, אֶלָּא שֶׁבְּכָל דּוֹר וָדוֹר, עוֹמְדִים עָלֵינוּ לְכַלּוֹתֵנוּ. וְהַקָּדוֹשׁ בָּרוּךְ הוּא מַצִּילֵנוּ מִיָּדָם:

מניחים את הכוס ומגלים את המצות.

צֵא וּלְמַד, מַה בִּקֵּשׁ לָבָן הָאֲרַמִּי לַעֲשׂוֹת לְיַעֲקֹב אָבִינוּ. שֶׁפַּרְעֹה לֹא גָזַר אֶלָּא עַל הַזְּכָרִים, וְלָבָן בִּקֵּשׁ לַעֲקֹר אֶת־הַכֹּל. שֶׁנֶּאֱמַר: אֲרַמִּי אֹבֵד אָבִי, וַיֵּרֶד מִצְרַיְמָה, וַיָּגָר שָׁם בִּמְתֵי מְעָט. וַיְהִי שָׁם לְגוֹי גָּדוֹל עָצוּם וָרָב:

Eliezer 48). It was she, still alive at the time of the Exodus, who remembered where Joseph's bones are buried so that Moses could fulfill Joseph's charge (*Mekhilta deRabbi Yishmael, Beshallah*). She was still alive at the time of David, and is identified as the "wise woman" who saved the town of Abel from being destroyed (*Midrash Samuel 32* on II Samuel 20). "Serah bat Asher, though hardly known, is a critical player in our nation's history – both as one who stirs the embers of our collective memory and as one who survives, undistinguished, as a source of continuity" (Rachel Adelman, *Serah bat Asher: Songstress, Poet, and Woman of Wisdom, Torah of the Mothers*).

Afterwards they shall leave with great riches

God commanded: "Each woman shall borrow from her neighbor and the lodger in her house objects of silver and gold, and clothing, and you shall put these on your sons and daughters, thus stripping the Egyptians" (*Exodus* 3:22). Why was this instruction given to the women, asks the Midrash. "Pharaoh had decreed that every

new-born male be thrown into the Nile. The daughters of Israel bribed Pharaoh's officials and the Egyptians drowned some of them and let others survive. This is why the text does not record that 'they threw every child.' The Holy One, blessed be He, therefore gave instructions that every woman shall ask back from her neighbor what had been taken in bribes. No deception was involved, only restitution" (*Midrash Hemdat Hayamim*).

Go forth and learn

Rabbi Joseph B. Soloveitchik, building on the view of the Hafetz Hayim, led those *gedolei Torah* of the past generation who encouraged advanced Torah and Talmud study for women. Rabbi Aharon Lichtenstein, *Rosh Yeshivat Har Etzion*, wrote that "it is desirable and necessary, not only possible, to provide intensive education for women from *Torah Shebe-al Pe* sources" (*Ten Da'at* 3:3), and the Lubavitcher Rebbe, Rabbi Menaham Schnerson, expressed a similarly positive attitude when he noted that current societal conditions demand that "not only is it *permitted* to teach wom-

The wine cup is raised and the matzot are covered.

This is what has stood by our ancestors and us! For not just one alone has risen against us to destroy us, but in every generation they rise against us to destroy us; and the Holy One, blessed be He, saves us from their hand!

The wine cup is put down and the matzot are uncovered.

Go forth and learn what Laban the Aramean wanted to do to our father Jacob. Pharaoh had decreed only against the males, but Laban wanted to uproot everyone – as it is said: "The Aramean wished to destroy my father; and he went down to Egypt and sojourned there, few in number; and he became there a nation – great and mighty and numerous."

---

en the Oral Torah, but, more than that, one *must* teach it to them…" (*Kefar Habad Newsletter*, 26 Iyyar 5750).

Indeed, we expect all our students to know the basics of a halakhic life style and to ask their *posek* when they do not know the answer to a complicated ques-

tion. But surely we consider it part of basic literacy for a yeshivah graduate – male or female – to be able look up something in the Mishnah Berurah before asking a question. Certainly we would not want to have teachers – male or female – who could not consult basic sources themselves and who

Rabbi Joseph B. Soloveitchik's inaugural Talmud shiur at the Stern College Beit Midrash.

Photo courtesy of Yeshiva University

וַיֵּרֶד מִצְרַיְמָה, אָנוּס עַל פִּי הַדִּבּוּר. וַיָּגָר שָׁם, מְלַמֵּד שֶׁלֹּא יָרַד יַעֲקֹב אָבִינוּ לְהִשְׁתַּקֵּעַ בְּמִצְרַיִם, אֶלָּא לָגוּר שָׁם, שֶׁנֶּאֱמַר: וַיֹּאמְרוּ אֶל־פַּרְעֹה, לָגוּר בָּאָרֶץ בָּאנוּ, כִּי אֵין מִרְעֶה לַצֹּאן אֲשֶׁר לַעֲבָדֶיךָ, כִּי כָבֵד הָרָעָב בְּאֶרֶץ כְּנָעַן. וְעַתָּה, יֵשְׁבוּ־נָא עֲבָדֶיךָ בְּאֶרֶץ גֹּשֶׁן:

בִּמְתֵי מְעָט, כְּמָה שֶׁנֶּאֱמַר: בְּשִׁבְעִים נֶפֶשׁ, יָרְדוּ אֲבֹתֶיךָ מִצְרָיְמָה. וְעַתָּה, שָׂמְךָ יְיָ אֱלֹהֶיךָ, כְּכוֹכְבֵי הַשָּׁמַיִם לָרֹב.

וַיְהִי שָׁם לְגוֹי, מְלַמֵּד שֶׁהָיוּ יִשְׂרָאֵל מְצֻיָּנִים שָׁם:

גָּדוֹל עָצוּם, כְּמָה שֶׁנֶּאֱמַר: וּבְנֵי יִשְׂרָאֵל, פָּרוּ וַיִּשְׁרְצוּ, וַיִּרְבּוּ וַיַּעַצְמוּ בִּמְאֹד מְאֹד, וַתִּמָּלֵא הָאָרֶץ אֹתָם:

וָרָב, כְּמָה שֶׁנֶּאֱמַר: רְבָבָה כְּצֶמַח הַשָּׂדֶה נְתַתִּיךְ, וַתִּרְבִּי, וַתִּגְדְּלִי,

---

could be counted on only to hand out the lists that either they themselves had copied when in school or had been handed by someone else. As women continue to take up senior positions in our educational institutions, we will expect them to have greater proficiency in all our classical sources.

Only against the males

The term "only" does not suggest that the decree against the males was comparatively insignificant. Rather, Exodus 1:10 makes clear that Pharaoh's chief motivation was to squelch any military threat that might emerge from the burgeoning Israelite population. Wanting only to maintain a military advantage and not "uproot everything," he targeted the newborn boys, the future soldiers. According to the Haggadah's reading of Deuteronomy 26:5, Lavan also sought the destruction of "only" a specific male,

and only one at that: he wished to absorb Ya'akov's household into his own idolatrous one, thereby uprooting the Jewish future on a spiritual plane (Laurie Novick).

Pharaoh deals in the currency of political power, while Lavan deals in the currency of women – namely, his two daughters. Leah and Rachel constitute valuable bargaining chips for their father (see *Genesis* 29:15–20) *and* his daughters recognize this (*Genesis* 31:15). Lavan mannages to barter his daughters in exchange for fourteen years of labor from Jacob. At the end of this time period, Lavan, having transacted a business deal, was to relinquish owner's rights over Rachel and Leah, yet he continues to claim rights to his daughters over Jacob. To illustrate this point, Lavan adamantly declares in Jacobs' presence that "the daughters are my daughters, and the sons are my sons, and the flocks are my flocks, and everything

"He went down to Egypt" – forced by Divine decree. "He sojourned there" – this teaches that our father Jacob did not go down to Egypt to settle, but only to live there temporarily. Thus it is said, "They said to Pharaoh, We have come to sojourn in the land, for there is no pasture for your servants' flocks because the hunger is severe in the land of Canaan; and now, please, let your servants dwell in the land of Goshen."

"Few in number" – as it is said: "Your ancestors went down to Egypt with seventy persons, and now, the Lord, your God, has made you as numerous as the stars of heaven."

"He became there a nation" – teaches that Israel was distinctive there.

"Great, mighty" – as it is said: "The children of Israel were fruitful and increased abundantly, and multiplied and became very, very mighty, and the land became filled with them."

"Numerous" – as it is said: "I caused you to thrive like the plants of the field, and you increased and grew and became very beautiful, your bosom fashioned and your hair grown long, but you were naked and

---

you see is mine" (*Genesis* 31:43). This curious possessive behavior echoes an earlier seemingly innocent sentiment expressed by Lavan as he greeted Jacob: "You are my bones and flesh" (*Genesis* 29:13). Lavan considers Jacob his own flesh and views Jacob's family as belonging to him and available to cater to his every whim. This is a dangerous family dynamic, one that reverses God's wish that "a man should leave his father and mother and cling to his wife that they may become one flesh" (*Genesis* 2:24).

"Go and learn" the threat of intra-family struggles, of domestic violence, and of the willingness to "sell" family members into situations which may not benefit them can "uproot the whole" and cause more profound damage that abuse of political power ever could (Rachel Brenner, *Columbia University Beit Midrash Haggadah*).

Goshen

The Midrash (*Pirkei de Rabbi Eliezer,* XXVI) teaches that when Sarah was in Egypt, Pharaoh drew up a marriage contract for her which included the gift of the land of Goshen. Though she refused him, he nonetheless gave her Goshen. It is because of her association with the city that Goshen was infused with an aura of holiness.

Thus the city's holiness precedes the inhabitance of the Children of Israel, just as the special nature of the entire nation is rooted in the past. It was not the Jews' function in Goshen to attempt to create holiness ex nihilo, but rather to actualize the holiness already infused in the soil by Sarah. It was her spirit which taught them of their past, their source, and, essentially, therefore, their present existence. It was not only their duty, therefore, but also

וָאֶעֱבֹר עָלַיִךְ וָאֶרְאֵךְ מִתְבּוֹסֶסֶת בְּדָמָיִךְ, וָאֹמַר לָךְ בְּדָמַיִךְ חֲיִי, וָאֹמַר לָךְ בְּדָמַיִךְ חֲיִי:

וַיָּרֵעוּ אֹתָנוּ הַמִּצְרִים וַיְעַנּוּנוּ, וַיִּתְּנוּ עָלֵינוּ עֲבֹדָה קָשָׁה:

וַיָּרֵעוּ אֹתָנוּ הַמִּצְרִים, כְּמָה שֶׁנֶּאֱמַר: הָבָה נִתְחַכְּמָה לוֹ. פֶּן־יִרְבֶּה, וְהָיָה כִּי־תִקְרֶאנָה מִלְחָמָה, וְנוֹסַף גַּם הוּא עַל־שֹׂנְאֵינוּ, וְנִלְחַם־בָּנוּ וְעָלָה מִן־הָאָרֶץ:

וַיְעַנּוּנוּ. כְּמָה שֶׁנֶּאֱמַר: וַיָּשִׂימוּ עָלָיו שָׂרֵי מִסִּים, לְמַעַן עַנֹּתוֹ בְּסִבְלֹתָם: וַיִּבֶן עָרֵי מִסְכְּנוֹת לְפַרְעֹה, אֶת־פִּתֹם וְאֶת־רַעַמְסֵס:

וַיִּתְּנוּ עָלֵינוּ עֲבֹדָה קָשָׁה, כְּמָה שֶׁנֶּאֱמַר: וַיַּעֲבִדוּ מִצְרַיִם אֶת־בְּנֵי יִשְׂרָאֵל בְּפָרֶךְ:

וַנִּצְעַק אֶל־יְיָ אֱלֹהֵי אֲבֹתֵינוּ, וַיִּשְׁמַע יְיָ אֶת־קֹלֵנוּ, וַיַּרְא אֶת־עָנְיֵנוּ, וְאֶת־עֲמָלֵנוּ, וְאֶת לַחֲצֵנוּ:

---

an existential imperative to actualize the spiritual potential created by the founders (Karin Rosenstock, *Columbia University Beit Midrash Haggadah*).

Va-rav – and great

The Haggadah's understanding of the words "*Va-rav* – and great" emphasizes the supernatural elements in the Jewish people's procreative abilities, and in the upbringing and survival of the Jewish children in Egypt. The prooftext brought in the Haggadah to support this idea comes from Ezekiel chapter 16, which includes a metaphorical description of God's loving protection of Jerusalem and which is the basis of the midrashic tradition (*TB*

Sotah 11b) that attributes the redemption from Egypt to the merit of the righteous women. God provided fish, a symbol of fertility, for the women in Egypt to urge the women to procreate. In return, when the women gave birth, God provided them with an angel as a midwife, and protected the babies until they could safely return home to their mothers. The Haggadah and the midrash in Sotah understood Ezekiel 16 as expressing the partnership which takes place in Egypt between Jewish women and God. The lesson of "*va-rav*" in the Haggadah is that while the women could not risk raising their own children, they still had the courage and faith in Hashem to go through with childbirth, to prove their

bare. I passed over you and saw you wallowing in your blood, and I said to you 'By your blood you shall live,' and I said to you 'By your blood you shall live!'"

"The Egyptians treated us badly and they made us suffer, and they put hard work upon us."

"The Egyptians treated us badly" – as it is said: "Come, let us act cunningly with them lest they multiply and, if there should be a war against us, they will join our enemies, fight against us and leave the land."

"They made us suffer" – as it is said: "They set taskmasters over [the people of Israel] to make them suffer with their burdens, and they built storage cities for Pharaoh, Pitom and Ramses."

"They put hard work upon us" – as it is said: "The Egyptians made the children of Israel work with rigor."

We cried out to the Lord, the God of our ancestors, and the Lord heard our voice and saw our suffering, our labor and our oppression.

"We cried out to the Lord, the God of our ancestors" – as it is said: "During that long period, the king of Egypt died; and the children of

---

subservience to God over Pharaoh. God's message in Ezekiel is one which we recite in the Haggadah and at every brit milah, *"be-damayikh hayi, be-damayikh hayi"* – a reminder that God joins Jewish parents in the nurturing and protection of our children (*Karen Miller*).

With rigor

Befarekh refers to the work beyond the normal standards of servitude. Nechama Leibowitz sees this concept further developed in the subsequent phrase (*Exodus* 1:14), "all of their work that they made them do was with rigor." This indicates that they were forced to do the work of the Egyptians ("their work"). The bitterness of the bondage in Egypt was heightened by the fact that they were oppressed not only by the

government, but also by all strata of Egyptian society (*Studies in the Haggadah from the Teachings of Nechama Leibowitz*).

We cried out to the Lord, the God of our ancestors

When the rabbis (*TB Berakhot* 31a–b) looked for a paradigm of true and authentic prayer, they turned to the prayer of Hanna, the mother of the prophet Samuel. Scrutinizing every detail of her prayer for a child (*1 Samuel* 1), they discovered the basic components of halakhic prayer. However, this story also forms an appropriate foreshadowing of the contemporary situation in the traditional Jewish community.

Hanna's story is well known. She was barren and suffering because of her barreness. Each year she would accompany

וַנִּצְעַק אֶל־יְיָ אֱלֹהֵי אֲבֹתֵינוּ, כְּמָה שֶׁנֶּאֱמַר: וַיְהִי בַיָּמִים הָרַבִּים הָהֵם, וַיָּמָת מֶלֶךְ מִצְרַיִם, וַיֵּאָנְחוּ בְנֵי־יִשְׂרָאֵל מִן־הָעֲבֹדָה וַיִּזְעָקוּ. וַתַּעַל שַׁוְעָתָם אֶל־הָאֱלֹהִים מִן־הָעֲבֹדָה:

וַיִּשְׁמַע יְיָ אֶת־קֹלֵנוּ, כְּמָה שֶׁנֶּאֱמַר: וַיִּשְׁמַע אֱלֹהִים אֶת־נַאֲקָתָם, וַיִּזְכֹּר אֱלֹהִים אֶת־בְּרִיתוֹ, אֶת־אַבְרָהָם, אֶת־יִצְחָק, וְאֶת־יַעֲקֹב:

וַיַּרְא אֶת־עָנְיֵנוּ. זוֹ פְּרִישׁוּת דֶּרֶךְ אֶרֶץ. כְּמָה שֶׁנֶּאֱמַר: וַיַּרְא אֱלֹהִים אֶת־בְּנֵי יִשְׂרָאֵל, וַיֵּדַע אֱלֹהִים:

---

her husband Elkana and his fertile second wife Penina to worship and offer sacrifice at Shilo. Each year she would be tormented to tears by Penina's taunts to the point where she could not eat. Frustrated by his inability to correct the situation, her husband Elkana said to her, "Hanna, why are you crying and why aren't you eating? Why are you so sad? Am I not more devoted to you than ten sons?"

Unconsoled, Hanna went to the sanctuary to pour out her heart to God. Eli the priest watched her, noticing that her lips were moving without making a sound. Regular worshipers, he knew, spoke their prayers aloud, so took her for a drunk. Eli said to her, "How long will you make a drunken spectacle of yourself? Sober up!" And Hanna replied, "Oh, no, my lord! I am a very unhappy woman. I have drunk no wine or other strong drink, but I have been pouring out my heart to the Lord...." "Then go in peace," said Eli, "and may the God of Israel grant what you have asked of Him."

At first glance, Elkana's consoling remarks are nothing but touching. He is fertile, as evidenced by Penina's children. He empathizes with her unfulfilled life, but can do nothing to help other than offering his devoted love and commitment. Malbim,

however, read Elkana's reaponse with a slightly different tone. Elkana is somewhat bewildered at Hanna's depression. There are only two reasons, he argues, for wanting children. One either wants to fulfill God's command to reproduce or fears facing old age without the support of children. Hanna (like all women) is not obligated in the mitzvah of reproduction; that obligation falls on men only. And as for the protection offered by one's children, he can provide the support of ten children. "Why are you crying and why aren't you eating?" he asks her. "Why are you so sad?"

His response, continues Malbim, drove Hanna to the sanctuary. She had never doubted the efficacy of prayer; but until then she had been relying on Elkana's prayers on her behalf. Once she realized that he could not feel her pain and hence could not advocate before God on her behalf, she went herself to pray in God's presence.

Eli, too, could not appreciate her predicament. Focusing on form, he noted that she has taken a non-traditional approach to prayer: speaking from the heart, not by way of her vocal chords. Having no other way of interpreting her action, he condemns her at first. But later, when he realizes her sincerity, he blesses her. "Then go in peace,"

Israel groaned because of the servitude, and they cried out. And their cry for help from their servitude rose up to God."

"The Lord heard our voice" – as it said: "God heard their groaning, and God remembered His covenant with Abraham, Isaac and Jacob."

"He saw our suffering" – this refers to the separation of husband and wife, as it is said: "God saw the children of Israel and God took note."

---

said Eli, "and may the God of Israel grant what you have asked of Him."

Motivated by their unprecedented high level of Jewish education, contemporary women have been expanding their participation in traditional religious life from which they heretofore have been excluded or exempted. Many religious leaders cannot understand the motivation for these innovations. Some respond with the voice of Elkana. There is no halakhic obligation for women to take on these additional roles; what positive agenda could motivate their demands. Have we not provided a positive religious community for men and women alike?

Others respond as did Eli. There is only one explanation for such non-traditional form, they argue. Only the heresies of religious reform and contemporary feminism could inspire these demands. These women must be drunk from the spirits of feminism; they should be admonished and rejected.

Indeed, modern halakhically committed Jews can find themselves more closely aligned with Eli than Elkana. Insensitivity to another's pain is intolerable, but that does not justify each and every personal response to such pain. As much as one might be interested in meeting the needs of another, halakhah provides a matrix within which one must work. Yet, as Eli found, not everything that seems out of step with traditional form is out of step

with halakhah. In fact, these new forms might well be the harbingers of enriching and religiously significant traditions.

Seeing past Elkana's insensitivity and avoiding falling into Eli's trap are no small feats. Differentiating between a voice expressed in the context of Torah and mitzvah, on the one hand, and one couched within a framework of halakhic indifference, on the other, takes time, calmness, and self-confidence.

God remembered His covenant with Abraham and Isaac and Jacob

The biblical verse (*Exodus* 2:24) uses the word *et* (*et* Avraham *et* Yitzhak *et* Ya'akov) to allude to the merits of the four matriarchs which God had also remembered (*Haggadat haRoke-ah*).

The disruption of normal family relations

When Pharaoh issued his decree against the unborn males, Amram was one of the leaders of the Jewish community. In response to that decree, he stopped having marital relations with his wife and divorced her. All of Israel then followed suit. Miriam reproved her father: "Your decree is harsher than Pharaoh's," she said, "for he decreed concerning only the males and you have decreed on male and female alike." He then took his wife back, as did the rest of the Jewish community. As a result, Moses was born (*Shemot Rabbah* 1)

וְאֶת־עֲמָלֵנוּ. אֵלּוּ הַבָּנִים. כְּמָה שֶׁנֶּאֱמַר: כָּל־הַבֵּן הַיִּלּוֹד הַיְאֹרָה תַּשְׁלִיכֻהוּ, וְכָל־הַבַּת תְּחַיּוּן:

וְאֶת לַחֲצֵנוּ. זֶה הַדְּחַק. כְּמָה שֶׁנֶּאֱמַר: וְגַם־רָאִיתִי אֶת־הַלַּחַץ, אֲשֶׁר מִצְרַיִם לֹחֲצִים אֹתָם:

וַיּוֹצִאֵנוּ יְיָ מִמִּצְרַיִם, בְּיָד חֲזָקָה, וּבִזְרֹעַ נְטוּיָה, וּבְמֹרָא גָּדֹל וּבְאֹתוֹת וּבְמֹפְתִים:

וַיּוֹצִאֵנוּ יְיָ מִמִּצְרַיִם. לֹא עַל־יְדֵי מַלְאָךְ, וְלֹא עַל־יְדֵי שָׂרָף, וְלֹא עַל־יְדֵי שָׁלִיחַ, אֶלָּא הַקָּדוֹשׁ בָּרוּךְ הוּא בִּכְבוֹדוֹ וּבְעַצְמוֹ. שֶׁנֶּאֱמַר: וְעָבַרְתִּי בְאֶרֶץ מִצְרַיִם בַּלַּיְלָה הַזֶּה, וְהִכֵּיתִי כָל־בְּכוֹר בְּאֶרֶץ מִצְרַיִם, מֵאָדָם וְעַד בְּהֵמָה, וּבְכָל־אֱלֹהֵי מִצְרַיִם אֶעֱשֶׂה שְׁפָטִים אֲנִי יְיָ:

וְעָבַרְתִּי בְאֶרֶץ־מִצְרַיִם בַּלַּיְלָה הַזֶּה, אֲנִי וְלֹא מַלְאָךְ. וְהִכֵּיתִי כָל בְּכוֹר בְּאֶרֶץ־מִצְרַיִם, אֲנִי וְלֹא שָׂרָף, וּבְכָל־אֱלֹהֵי מִצְרַיִם אֶעֱשֶׂה שְׁפָטִים, אֲנִי וְלֹא הַשָּׁלִיחַ. אֲנִי יְיָ, אֲנִי הוּא וְלֹא אַחֵר:

Miriam is also responsible for the emergence of Moses as a leader and redeemer of his people, writes Rabbi Joseph B. Soloveitchik. "If not for her, he would have never been imbued with great passionate love for his poor brethren. She suggested to the princess that a Hebrew wet-nurse be employed for the infant (*Exodus 2:4,7,8*), preventing Moses from disappearing in anonymity and ignorance" (*Family Redeemed*).

Every boy born should be thrown in the river

Shifra and Puah, the two midwives who feared God and defied Pharaoh's order to kill all the male Jewish babies (*Exodus 1:15–17*), are traditionally identified as either Yocheved and her daughter Miriam or Yocheved and her daughter-in-law Elisheva, Aharon's wife (*TB Sotah 11b*). However, Nechama Leibowitz quotes a tradition that the midwives were Egyptians who eventually converted to Judaism. After all, how could Pharaoh have possibly expected Jewish women to carry out such an order?

Midrash Tadesh (21) lists twenty-two saintly Jewish women, followed by their "gentile proselyte" counterparts: Hagar, Zipporah, Shifra, Puah, Pharaoh's daughter Bitya, Rahab, Ruth, and Yael. This indicates how the individual can resist evil, writes Nechama (the "title" by which she preferred to be addressed by her students). "The text

"Our labor" – this refers to the "children," as it is said: "Every boy that is born, you shall throw into the river and every girl you shall keep alive."

"Our oppression" – this refers to the pressure, as it is said: "I have seen the oppression with which the Egyptians oppress them."

"The Lord took us out of Egypt with a strong hand and an outstretched arm, and with a great manifestation, and with signs and wonders."

"The Lord took us out of Egypt" – not using an angel, not using a *seraph* and not using a messenger. The Holy One, blessed be He, did it in His glory by Himself!

Thus it is said: "In that night I will pass through the land of Egypt, and I will smite every first-born in the land of Egypt, from man to beast, and I will carry out judgments against all the gods of Egypt, I the Lord."

"I will pass through the land of Egypt" – I and not an angel; "I will smite every first-born in the land of Egypt" – I and not a *seraph*; "I will carry out judgments against all the gods of Egypt" – I and not a messenger; "I the Lord" – it is I, and none other!

---

contrasts the brutal decrees of enslavement and massacre initiated by Pharaoh and supported by government and people with the God-fearing 'civil disobedience' of the midwives. Neither moral courage nor sheer wickedness is an ethnically or nationally determined quality. Moab and Amnon produced a Ruth and Naamah [mother of Rehoboam and the ancestress of Isaiah the prophet], respectively, Egypt two righteous midwives" (*New Studies in Shemot*).

The first two letters of Yocheved and the last two of Bitya evoke God's name. These two women are Moses' biological and adopted mothers, respectively, and their names and actions, she suggests, remind us of Mother *Shekhinah*, the Divine Presence which came to join these two women to protect Moses as he grew (Lea Gerber).

"Whenever Rav Yosef head the foot-steps of his mother, he would say, 'Let me rise because the *Shekhinah* is coming" (*TB Kiddushin* 31b). "If the *Shekhinah* is here," says Rabbi Joseph B. Soloveitchik, "if She is like a good loving mother who holds us in her embrace, cares for us, is concerned about us and never absents herself from us – then She expects reciprocity. The wish of Mother *Shekhinah* should not be ignored. One must quest for Her, search for Her. One will finally find Her if the questing is sincere and genuine" (*Family Redeemed*).

Every daughter you shall keep alive
Pharaoh dismisses the daughters as insignificant, almost useless. Yet, in the very next verse we read that Levi's daughter conceives and cleverly hides the child who will eventually undo Pharaoh's decree. Her own daughter Miriam keeps close watch

בְּיָד חֲזָקָה. זוֹ הַדֶּבֶר, כְּמָה שֶׁנֶּאֱמַר: הִנֵּה יַד־יְיָ הוֹיָה, בְּמִקְנְךָ אֲשֶׁר בַּשָּׂדֶה, בַּסּוּסִים בַּחֲמֹרִים בַּגְּמַלִּים, בַּבָּקָר וּבַצֹּאן, דֶּבֶר כָּבֵד מְאֹד:

וּבִזְרֹעַ נְטוּיָה. זוֹ הַחֶרֶב. כְּמָה שֶׁנֶּאֱמַר: וְחַרְבּוֹ שְׁלוּפָה בְּיָדוֹ, נְטוּיָה עַל־יְרוּשָׁלָיִם:

וּבְמֹרָא גָּדוֹל. זֶה גִּלּוּי שְׁכִינָה, כְּמָה שֶׁנֶּאֱמַר: אוֹ הֲנִסָּה אֱלֹהִים, לָבוֹא לָקַחַת לוֹ גוֹי מִקֶּרֶב גּוֹי, בְּמַסֹּת בְּאֹתֹת וּבְמוֹפְתִים וּבְמִלְחָמָה, וּבְיָד חֲזָקָה וּבִזְרֹעַ נְטוּיָה, וּבְמוֹרָאִים גְּדֹלִים. כְּכֹל אֲשֶׁר־עָשָׂה לָכֶם יְיָ אֱלֹהֵיכֶם בְּמִצְרַיִם, לְעֵינֶיךָ:

וּבְאֹתוֹת. זֶה הַמַּטֶּה, כְּמָה שֶׁנֶּאֱמַר: וְאֶת הַמַּטֶּה הַזֶּה תִּקַּח בְּיָדֶךָ. אֲשֶׁר תַּעֲשֶׂה־בּוֹ אֶת־הָאֹתֹת:

וּבְמֹפְתִים. זֶה הַדָּם, כְּמָה שֶׁנֶּאֱמַר: וְנָתַתִּי מוֹפְתִים, בַּשָּׁמַיִם וּבָאָרֶץ:

במילים "דם ואש ותימרות עשן" מטיפים מעט יין מן הכוס.

דָּם, וָאֵשׁ, וְתִימְרוֹת עָשָׁן:

דָּבָר אַחֵר: בְּיָד חֲזָקָה שְׁתַּיִם. וּבִזְרֹעַ נְטוּיָה שְׁתַּיִם. וּבְמֹרָא גָּדוֹל שְׁתַּיִם. וּבְאֹתוֹת שְׁתַּיִם. וּבְמֹפְתִים שְׁתַּיִם:

אֵלּוּ עֶשֶׂר מַכּוֹת שֶׁהֵבִיא הַקָּדוֹשׁ בָּרוּךְ הוּא עַל־הַמִּצְרִים בְּמִצְרַיִם, וְאֵלּוּ הֵן:

בכל מכה ומכה וכן במילים דצ"ך עד"ש באח"ב מטיפים מעט יין מן הכוס.

דָּם, צְפַרְדֵּעַ, כִּנִּים, עָרוֹב, דֶּבֶר, שְׁחִין, בָּרָד, אַרְבֶּה, חֹשֶׁךְ, מַכַּת בְּכוֹרוֹת:

on her brother and suggests the brilliant adoption plan. And it is Pharaoh's very own daughter who defies her father and saves the life of the child. Thus we may

"With a strong hand" – this refers to the *dever* (pestilence) as it is said: "Behold, the hand of the Lord will be upon your livestock in the field, upon the horses, the donkeys, the camels, the herds and the flocks, a very severe pestilence."

"With an outstretched arm" – this refers to the sword, as it is said: "His sword was drawn, in his hand, stretched out over Jerusalem."

"With a great manifestation" – this refers to the revelation of the *Shekhinah* (Divine Presence), as it is said: "Has any God ever tried to take for himself a nation from the midst of another nation, with trials, signs and wonders, with war and with a strong hand and an outstretched arm, and with great manifestations, like all that the Lord your God, did for you in Egypt before your eyes!"

"With signs" – this refers to the staff, as it is said: "Take into your hand this staff with which you shall perform the signs."

"Wonders" – this refers to the blood, as it is said: "I shall show wonders in heaven and on earth."

Some wine is spilled from the cup during the recitation of the words "blood, and fire, and pillars of smoke."

Blood, and fire, and pillars of smoke.

Another explanation: "Strong hand" indicates two [plagues]; "Outstretched arm," another two; "Great manifestation," another two; "Signs," another two; and "Wonders," another two.

These are the Ten Plagues which the Holy One, blessed be He, brought upon the Egyptians, namely as follows:

Some wine is spilled from the cup during the recitation of each of the ten plagues.

Blood. Frogs. Lice. Wild Beasts. Pestilence. Boils. Hail. Locust. Darkness. Smiting the First-born.

---

read the text as an unwitting prophecy on Pharaoh's part: "All the daughters will sustain life" (Esther Lapian).

Blood

The Nile turning to blood was a nightmare for the Egyptians, and like many night-

רַבִּי יְהוּדָה הָיָה נוֹתֵן בָּהֶם סִמָּנִים:
דְּצַ"ךְ, עֲדַ"שׁ, בְּאַחַ"ב:

רַבִּי יוֹסֵי הַגְּלִילִי אוֹמֵר: מִנַּיִן אַתָּה אוֹמֵר, שֶׁלָּקוּ הַמִּצְרִים
בְּמִצְרַיִם עֶשֶׂר מַכּוֹת, וְעַל הַיָּם לָקוּ חֲמִשִּׁים מַכּוֹת? בְּמִצְרַיִם
מָה הוּא אוֹמֵר: וַיֹּאמְרוּ הַחַרְטֻמִּם אֶל־פַּרְעֹה, אֶצְבַּע אֱלֹהִים
הִיא. וְעַל הַיָּם מָה הוּא אוֹמֵר? וַיַּרְא יִשְׂרָאֵל אֶת־הַיָּד הַגְּדֹלָה,
אֲשֶׁר עָשָׂה יְיָ בְּמִצְרַיִם, וַיִּירְאוּ הָעָם אֶת־יְיָ. וַיַּאֲמִינוּ בַּיָי, וּבְמֹשֶׁה

mares, it was a grotesque and frightening distortion of a common sight. The Egyptians watched with equanimity as newborn babies thrown into the Nile bloodied the waters with prenatal blood. Now that blood spreads towards them when they try to drink from the river (*Hayuta Deutch, Kolekh*, no. 5).

Frogs
The Egyptians had feared the abundant increase (*va-yishreztu*, Exodus 1:7) of the Jews and reacted inhumanely. They were punished with the uncontrolled swarming – *ve-sharatz haye'or* (Exodus 7:28) – of the frogs (*Hayuta Deutch, Koleikh*, no. 5).

Killing of the First-Born
Bitya, first born to Pharaoh, was spared because she had saved Moses when he was a baby (*Exodus* 2:6). "She girds herself with strength...she rises while it is still night" (*Proverbs* 31:15, 17) – this was the night when the first-born were killed, as the Midrash suggests (*Exodus Rabbah* 18:3).

Rabbi Yosi HaGelili said
I never understood these passages of the Haggadah until I read Leon Wieseltier's book *Kaddish*. "The promise of salvation is always a specific promise. A general promise is never enough.... The more you suffer,

the more vividly you imagine the end of your suffering... There is no more evidence for a general promise than for a particular promise. These are all undisciplined ideas. So why not picture happiness in its particulars?" Delving into the meaning of Rabbi Yossi's five-fingered hand of plagues or searching the Tanakh to find justification of Rabbi Akiva's two hundred and fifty miracles would be missing the point. The nation's suffering in slavery precipitated a need to quantify salvation, to find in numbers the relief that the exile was near its end. The escalated numbers are a statement of the majesty of the Exodus in all of its particulars. Those particulars may exist on the page, or they may exist more powerfully in the imagination. Fifty, two hundred or two-hundred-fifty are not merely numbers; they are happy equations of salvation (Erica Brown, *A Celebration of the Haggadah*, The Women's Beit Midrash).

Our desire to see that there were more and more plagues inflicted on the Egyptians is not an expression of hate for them but rather an appreciation of God's control of the natural order of the world and His ability to change it. The plagues are a parallel to the miracles mentioned in the *Dayenu* prayer that immediately follows, both expressions of God's powers over both hu-

Rabbi Yehudah referred to them by acronyms:

DeTzaKh (blood, frogs, lice); *ADaSh* (beasts, pestilence, boils); *BeAHaV* (hail, locust, darkness, first-born).

Rabbi Yossi the Gallilean said: How do you know that the Egyptians were stricken by ten plagues in Egypt, and then were struck by fifty plagues at the sea? In Egypt it says of them, "The magicians said to Pharaoh 'This is the finger of God.' At the sea it says, "Israel saw the great hand that the Lord laid against Egypt; and the people feared the Lord, and they believed in the Lord and in His servant Moses." Now,

---

man life and nature. The plagues may have been aimed at the Egyptians on a physical level, but their message was also for the Jews: Hashem has power far greater than that of the mighty Egyptian court, and He would protect them. The Rabbis wanted us to appreciate each and every miracle mentioned in the *Dayenu*, as well as each Divine power used to create both those miracles and the extraordinary plagues. That appreciation became an enhanced faith in God and His powers, bolstered by God's mastery over the awesome enslaving regime – as evidenced visually by the plagues and miracles – and the basis for belief that continues unto this very day (Frieda R. Feldman Horwitz).

This section is not included in the Rambam's Haggadah, his son reports (*quoted in Haggadah Sheleima*), because it was not widespread throughout the various communities and was therefore not part of the required recitation. Nevertheless, the Rambam himself recited it at his own *seder*, and it is a model of the play of numbers in the text that engage those who love the texts they study.

Rabbanit Rivka Segal, wife of Rabbi David Halevi, the author of the *Turei Zahav* (*Taz*), and daughter of Rabbi Yoel Sirkes, author of the *Bayit Hadash* (*Bah*), was one of those people who took an interest in the

numbers concerning the texts she studied. When she was twelve years old, some of her father's students were eating the Shabbat meal with the family and in the course of their Torah discussions asked her what ten-letter word is found in the Torah. She quickly replied that there is no ten-letter word in the Torah, but there is one in the Prophets: "*lemishpehoteihem*" (*Joshua* 12:21). After a moment's thought, she added that there is a twelve-letter word in the Book of Esther (9:3): "*veha'arhashdarpanim*" (Shelomo Ashkenazi, *Ha-Isha be-Aspaklarit ha-Yehudit*).

They believed in the Lord and in His servant Moses

In the Bible, this sentence, the only actual reference to Moses, Aaron or Miriam in the Haggadah, introduces the triumphant *Shirat haYam*, the Song at the Sea (*Exodus* 15:1–18), sung by Moses and the Israelites at the Red Sea: "I will sing to the Lord for He is highly exalted; the horse and the rider has He thrown into the sea."

In response to this celebration of the miracle of deliverance at the Red Sea, "Miriam the prophetess, the sister of Aaron, took a timbrel in her hand; and all the women went out after her with timbrels and with dances. And Miriam sang to them, 'Sing to the Lord for He is highly exalted; the horse

עַבְדוֹ: כַּמָּה לָקוּ בְּאֶצְבַּע? עֶשֶׂר מַכּוֹת. אֱמוֹר מֵעַתָּה: בְּמִצְרַיִם לָקוּ עֶשֶׂר מַכּוֹת, וְעַל־הַיָּם לָקוּ חֲמִשִּׁים מַכּוֹת:

רַבִּי אֱלִיעֶזֶר אוֹמֵר: מִנַּיִן שֶׁכָּל־מַכָּה וּמַכָּה, שֶׁהֵבִיא הַקָּדוֹשׁ בָּרוּךְ הוּא עַל הַמִּצְרִים בְּמִצְרַיִם, הָיְתָה שֶׁל אַרְבַּע מַכּוֹת? שֶׁנֶּאֱמַר: יְשַׁלַּח־בָּם חֲרוֹן אַפּוֹ, עֶבְרָה וָזַעַם וְצָרָה, מִשְׁלַחַת מַלְאֲכֵי רָעִים: עֶבְרָה אַחַת. וָזַעַם שְׁתַּיִם. וְצָרָה שָׁלֹשׁ. מִשְׁלַחַת מַלְאֲכֵי רָעִים אַרְבַּע. אֱמוֹר מֵעַתָּה: בְּמִצְרַיִם לָקוּ אַרְבָּעִים מַכּוֹת, וְעַל הַיָּם לָקוּ מָאתַיִם מַכּוֹת:

רַבִּי עֲקִיבָא אוֹמֵר: מִנַּיִן שֶׁכָּל־מַכָּה וּמַכָּה, שֶׁהֵבִיא הַקָּדוֹשׁ בָּרוּךְ הוּא עַל הַמִּצְרִים בְּמִצְרַיִם, הָיְתָה שֶׁל חָמֵשׁ מַכּוֹת? שֶׁנֶּאֱמַר: יְשַׁלַּח־בָּם חֲרוֹן אַפּוֹ, עֶבְרָה וָזַעַם וְצָרָה, מִשְׁלַחַת מַלְאֲכֵי רָעִים: חֲרוֹן אַפּוֹ אַחַת. עֶבְרָה שְׁתַּיִם. וָזַעַם שָׁלֹשׁ. וְצָרָה אַרְבַּע. מִשְׁלַחַת מַלְאֲכֵי רָעִים חָמֵשׁ. אֱמוֹר מֵעַתָּה: בְּמִצְרַיִם לָקוּ חֲמִשִּׁים מַכּוֹת, וְעַל הַיָּם לָקוּ חֲמִשִּׁים וּמָאתַיִם מַכּוֹת.

---

and the rider has He thrown into the sea'" (*Exodus* 15:20–21).

Where did they get timbrels at the sea, asks the Midrash. Miriam had them ready because the righteous, having seen the miracles in Egypt, anticipated the deliverance and had prepared them for the people (*Mekhilta deRabbi Yishmael, Beshalah* 10).

"Miriam the prophetess" is referred to as "the sister of Aaron" and not "the sister of Aaron and Moses" because her first prophecy preceded Moses' birth, when she was only Aaron's sister. "She prophesied that her mother would give birth to a son who would be the savior of Israel. When Moses was born, the house filled with light; her father then stood and kissed her on the head, saying, 'My daughter, your prophecy has been fulfilled'" (*TB Megilla* 14a).

Paralleling Moses' victory song is *Shirat Devorah* (*Judges* 5), the celebration of the victory of Devorah, the prophet who was a Judge of Israel. "She sat under the palm tree of Devorah between Ramah and Beit-El in the hill country of Ephraim, and the Children of Israel came to her for judgment" (*Judges* 4:4). She summoned Barak to be her commander to fight Sisera, the head of the army of Jabin, king of Canaan, who then ruled over the Jews. She went with him to lead the battle, "for the Lord will give Sisera over into the hands of a woman" (v. 9). *Shirat Devorah* is read as the *haftara* for *Beshalah*, which contains *Shirat haYam*. They are both written according to the same layout, with blank spaces above and below the written phrases.

Miriam and Devorah are not the only

how often were they smitten by 'the finger'? Ten plagues! Thus you must conclude that in Egypt they were smitten by ten plagues, at the sea they were smitten by fifty plagues!

Rabbi Eliezer said: How do we know that each individual plague which the Holy One, blessed be He, brought upon the Egyptians in Egypt consisted of four plagues? For it is said: "He sent against them His fierce anger, fury, and indignation, and trouble, a discharge of messengers of evil": 'Fury,' is one; 'Indignation,' makes two; 'Trouble,' makes three; 'Discharge of messengers of evil,' makes four. Thus you must now say that in Egypt they were struck by forty plagues, and at the sea they were stricken by two hundred plagues.

Rabbi Akiva said: How do we know that each individual plague which the Holy One, blessed be He, brought upon the Egyptians in Egypt consisted of five plagues? For it is said: "He sent against them his fierce anger, fury, and indignation, and trouble, a discharge of messengers of evil": "His fierce anger," is one; "fury," makes two; "indignation," makes three; "trouble," makes four; "discharge of messengers of evil," makes five. Thus you must now say that in Egypt they were struck by fifty plagues, and at the sea they were stricken by two hundred and fifty plagues.

---

two women biblical personalities who reached the status of prophet. The Talmud (TB *Megilla* 14a) lists five others: Sarah, Hannah, Avigayil, Hulda and Esther. Other midrashim add the other Matriarchs – Rivka, Rahel and Leah – as well as Hagar, Serah bat Asher, Bitya (Pharaoh's daughter) and Bat Sheva. Rabbenu Bahya quoted Rabbi Helbo to the effect that there were thousands of both male and female prophets (*Shir haShirim Rabbah* 4).

"The mere fact that among our prophets we find women to whom God has addressed Himself," writes Rabbi Joseph B. Soloveitchik, "is clear proof that we never differentiated between the sexes axiologically." Indeed, he writes, "the uniqueness of man is expressed in passional experiences, in his ability to withdraw from positions conquered, in his readiness to sacrifice and to make the movement of recoil, in his giving himself to others, in his craving, as a lonely being, for communion with God; therefore, there is hardly any cogent reason to place the worth of man above that of the female. On the contrary, sacrificial, passional action is more characteristic of the woman than of man" (*Family Redeemed*).

The prophetess Avigayil was the wife of Nabal the Carmelite. When David was about to kill Nabal in response to his refusal to repay David for having protected his property, Avigayil shrewdly and boldly approached David and pleaded successfully on his behalf. When God struck Nabal a

כַּמָּה מַעֲלוֹת טוֹבוֹת לַמָּקוֹם עָלֵינוּ:

אִלּוּ הוֹצִיאָנוּ מִמִּצְרַיִם, וְלֹא עָשָׂה בָהֶם שְׁפָטִים, דַּיֵּנוּ:

אִלּוּ עָשָׂה בָהֶם שְׁפָטִים, וְלֹא עָשָׂה בֵאלֹהֵיהֶם, דַּיֵּנוּ:

אִלּוּ עָשָׂה בֵאלֹהֵיהֶם, וְלֹא הָרַג אֶת־בְּכוֹרֵיהֶם, דַּיֵּנוּ:

אִלּוּ הָרַג אֶת־בְּכוֹרֵיהֶם, וְלֹא נָתַן לָנוּ אֶת־מָמוֹנָם, דַּיֵּנוּ:

אִלּוּ נָתַן לָנוּ אֶת־מָמוֹנָם, וְלֹא קָרַע לָנוּ אֶת־הַיָּם, דַּיֵּנוּ:

אִלּוּ קָרַע לָנוּ אֶת־הַיָּם, וְלֹא הֶעֱבִירָנוּ בְתוֹכוֹ בֶּחָרָבָה, דַּיֵּנוּ:

אִלּוּ הֶעֱבִירָנוּ בְתוֹכוֹ בֶּחָרָבָה, וְלֹא שִׁקַּע צָרֵינוּ בְּתוֹכוֹ, דַּיֵּנוּ:

אִלּוּ שִׁקַּע צָרֵינוּ בְּתוֹכוֹ, וְלֹא סִפֵּק צָרְכֵּנוּ בַּמִּדְבָּר אַרְבָּעִים שָׁנָה, דַּיֵּנוּ:

---

short time later, David proposed to her and took her as one of his wives (*II Samuel* 2–41). Avigayil – along with Sarah, Rahav and Esther – is also counted among the most beautiful women in the world (*TB Megilla* 15a).

Hulda is introduced in the Book of Kings: "So Hilkiyahu the priest and Ahikam and Akhbor and Shfan and Asaya went to Hulda the prophetess, the wife of Shallum the son of Tikva the son of Harhas, keeper of the wardrobe. She dwelt in Jerusalem, 'in the *mishne*,' and they spoke to her" (*II Kings* 22:14). "In the *mishne*" refers to a geographical location, "in the second quarter of the city." But Rashi translates it otherwise: She taught the oral law to the elders of the generation, and that is the *mishne*. She taught from the beginning to the end of Deuteronomy (*Mishne Torah*). And all the extra words of the Torah she exounded upon in public. She revealed the punishments and the exiles that would be multiplied for those who transgress the secrets and the hints of the Torah. Ralbag notes that Targum Yonatan translates "in the *mishne*" as "in the house of study." Hulda

was thereby a source of Torah, a teacher, and a prophet.

Yael Levine (*Da'at* no. 44) notes that the kabbalists associated the list of seven women prophets with the seven kabbalistic *sefirot*. The earliest known mention of the correlation between the prophetesses and the *Sefirot* appears in Bahya's commentary on the Pentateuch to the song of Miriam (*Exodus* 15:20), and has been articulated in literature of varying types, among them kabbalistic, midrashic, and hasidic commentaries.

Dayenu

How can we really say "*Dayenu* – it would have been enough for us"? We needed each and every one of these events! Rather, we are saying that each time God performed one miracle for us, we thought it could not get any better. Once the next miracle was performed, the preceding one was, of course, known to not have been enough; but the following miracle was not even conceivable and its lack was not felt (Dassi Tropper, *Yeshivat Ramaz Likrat Shabbat Haggadah*).

How many levels of favors has the Omnipresent One bestowed upon us:

If He had only brought us out from Egypt, and had not carried out judgments against them, *Dayenu*, it would have sufficed us!

If He had only carried out judgments against them, and not against their idols, *Dayenu*, it would have sufficed us!

If He had only destroyed their idols, and had not smitten their first-born, *Dayenu*, it would have sufficed us!

If He had only smitten their first-born, and had not given us their wealth, *Dayenu*, it would have sufficed us!

If He had only given us their wealth, and had not split the sea for us, *Dayenu*, it would have sufficed us!

If He had only split the sea for us, and had not taken us through it on dry land, *Dayenu*, it would have sufficed us!

If He had only taken us through the sea on dry land, and had not drowned our oppressors in it, *Dayenu*, it would have sufficed us!

If He had only drowned our oppressors in it, and had not supplied our needs in the desert for forty years, *Dayenu*, it would have sufficed us!

The cleverness of the poem lies in its ability to generate an experiential quality, a critical concern of the *seder* itself. The reader is told that the following is a list of the "good steps" God has led the Jews through, and is then led through them herself as she experiences the step-like structure of the poem. Each act becomes uniquely important as it takes its turn in the formulaic phrasing and is capped with the resolute "*Dayenu.*" The counting device imbues each act with its own weight and import (Shulie Rubin, *Columbia University Beit Midrash Haggadah*).

If He had only taken us through the sea on dry land but had not drowned our oppressors

All of Israel recognized God's hand in their salvation at the Sea, but, says Avivah Gottlieb Zornberg, the women enjoyed a special insight. When the Israelite women had come to give birth in Egypt, says the Talmud (*BT Sota* 11b), they did so in the field. The women felt not only the shadow of death that hovers over all births, but the added fear of discovery by the Egyptians who had set themselves against babies and birth. At that time, continues the Talmud, God sent one from the highest heavens to clean and tend to them, like a midwife. So when God appeared to them at the Sea, they were the first to recognize Him, as it is said, "This is my God..." (*Exodus* 15:2). Another source (*Midrash Rabbah* 23:8), she notes, has God Himself acting as the midwife.

"The women recognize their midwife when God appears over the Red Sea; what they have experienced of love and care in their own moment of crossing – at the breaking of their own waters – becomes a

אִלּוּ סִפֵּק צָרְכֵּנוּ בַּמִּדְבָּר אַרְבָּעִים שָׁנָה, וְלֹא הֶאֱכִילָנוּ
אֶת־הַמָּן, דַּיֵּנוּ:

אִלּוּ הֶאֱכִילָנוּ אֶת־הַמָּן, וְלֹא נָתַן לָנוּ אֶת־הַשַּׁבָּת, דַּיֵּנוּ:

אִלּוּ נָתַן לָנוּ אֶת־הַשַּׁבָּת, וְלֹא קֵרְבָנוּ לִפְנֵי הַר סִינַי, דַּיֵּנוּ:

אִלּוּ קֵרְבָנוּ לִפְנֵי הַר סִינַי, וְלֹא נָתַן לָנוּ אֶת־הַתּוֹרָה, דַּיֵּנוּ:

אִלּוּ נָתַן לָנוּ אֶת־הַתּוֹרָה, וְלֹא הִכְנִיסָנוּ לְאֶרֶץ יִשְׂרָאֵל, דַּיֵּנוּ:

אִלּוּ הִכְנִיסָנוּ לְאֶרֶץ יִשְׂרָאֵל, וְלֹא בָנָה לָנוּ אֶת־בֵּית הַבְּחִירָה, דַּיֵּנוּ:

עַל אַחַת כַּמָּה וְכַמָּה טוֹבָה כְפוּלָה וּמְכֻפֶּלֶת לַמָּקוֹם עָלֵינוּ: שֶׁהוֹצִיאָנוּ מִמִּצְרַיִם, וְעָשָׂה בָהֶם שְׁפָטִים, וְעָשָׂה בֵאלֹהֵיהֶם, וְהָרַג אֶת־בְּכוֹרֵיהֶם, וְנָתַן לָנוּ אֶת־מָמוֹנָם, וְקָרַע לָנוּ אֶת־הַיָּם, וְהֶעֱבִירָנוּ בְתוֹכוֹ בֶחָרָבָה, וְשִׁקַּע צָרֵינוּ בְּתוֹכוֹ, וְסִפֵּק צָרְכֵּנוּ בַּמִּדְבָּר אַרְבָּעִים שָׁנָה, וְהֶאֱכִילָנוּ אֶת־הַמָּן, וְנָתַן לָנוּ אֶת־הַשַּׁבָּת, וְקֵרְבָנוּ לִפְנֵי הַר סִינַי, וְנָתַן לָנוּ אֶת־הַתּוֹרָה, וְהִכְנִיסָנוּ לְאֶרֶץ יִשְׂרָאֵל, וּבָנָה לָנוּ אֶת־בֵּית הַבְּחִירָה, לְכַפֵּר עַל־כָּל־עֲוֹנוֹתֵינוּ.

רַבָּן גַּמְלִיאֵל הָיָה אוֹמֵר: כָּל שֶׁלֹּא אָמַר שְׁלֹשָׁה דְבָרִים אֵלּוּ בַּפֶּסַח, לֹא יָצָא יְדֵי חוֹבָתוֹ, וְאֵלּוּ הֵן:
פֶּסַח, מַצָּה, וּמָרוֹר:

key to understanding the miracle at the Sea. From their most intimate knowledge of the verge, the seam joining life and death, they are the first to know the God who splits the waters and brings life through to another shore" (*The Particulars of Rapture*).

If He had only supplied our needs in the desert for forty years and not fed us the manna
R. Yose ben Yehuda said, "Three good leaders have arisen for Israel; they are Moses,

Aaron, and Miriam. And three precious gifts were presented to Israel for their sake: These are the well, the pillar of cloud, and the manna. The well was given for the merits of Miriam, the pillar for the merits of Aaron, and the manna for the merits of Moses" (*TB Ta'anit* 9a).

If He had only given us the Torah and not brought us into the Land of Israel
For the Satmar Rav, Rabbi Yoel Teitlebaum,

If He had only supplied our needs in the desert for forty years, and had
not fed us the manna, *Dayenu*, it would have sufficed us!

If He had only fed us the manna, and had not given us the Shabbat,
Dayenu, it would have sufficed us!

If He had only given us the Shabbat, and had not brought us before
Mount Sinai, *Dayenu*, it would have sufficed us!

If He had only brought us before Mount Sinai, and had not given us
the Torah, *Dayenu*, it would have sufficed us!

If He had only given us the Torah, and had not brought us into the
land of Israel, *Dayenu*, it would have sufficed us!

If He had only brought us into the land of Israel, and had not built for
us the Temple, the Chosen House, *Dayenu*, it would have sufficed
us!

Thus how much more so should we be grateful to the Omnipresent
One for the doubled and redoubled goodness that He has bestowed
upon us; for He brought us out of Egypt, and carried out judgments
against them, and against their idols, and smote their first-born, and
gave us their wealth, and split the sea for us, and took us through it on
dry land, and drowned our oppressors in it, and supplied our needs in
the desert for forty years, and fed us the manna, and gave us the Shabbat, and brought us before Mount Sinai, and gave us the Torah, and
brought us into the land of Israel and built for us the Chosen House
to atone for all our sins.

Rabban Gamliel used to say: Whoever does not discuss the following
three things on Passover has not fulfilled his duty, namely:
Pesah (the Passover-sacrifice), *Matzah* (the unleavened bread), and *Maror* (the bitter herbs).

---

the Haggadah tells us that "it would have
been enough if He had given us the Torah
and not brought us to the Land of Israel" in
order to discredit the secular Zionists who
would themselves set up a Jewish State in
the Land of Israel (*Haggadat Mahari Tab*).

But others understand that the humans
involved in establishing the State were but
God's agents: "I do not know whom the

journalists, with their human eyes, saw
sitting in the chairman's seat during that
fateful session when the General Assembly
decided in favor of the establishment of the
State," writes Rabbi Joseph B. Soloveitchik.
"However, someone who at that time observed with his spiritual eyes could have
sensed the presence of the true Chairman
who presided over the discussion – the

כשאומרים "פסח שהיו אבותינו אוכלים", לא מגביהים את התבשיל.

פֶּסַח שֶׁהָיוּ אֲבוֹתֵינוּ אוֹכְלִים, בִּזְמַן שֶׁבֵּית הַמִּקְדָּשׁ הָיָה קַיָּם, עַל שׁוּם מָה? עַל שׁוּם שֶׁפָּסַח הַקָּדוֹשׁ בָּרוּךְ הוּא, עַל בָּתֵּי אֲבוֹתֵינוּ בְּמִצְרַיִם, שֶׁנֶּאֱמַר: וַאֲמַרְתֶּם זֶבַח פֶּסַח הוּא לַיְיָ, אֲשֶׁר פָּסַח עַל בָּתֵּי בְנֵי יִשְׂרָאֵל בְּמִצְרַיִם בְּנָגְפּוֹ אֶת־מִצְרַיִם, וְאֶת־בָּתֵּינוּ הִצִּיל, וַיִּקֹּד הָעָם וַיִּשְׁתַּחֲווּ:

מגביהים את המצה ומראים למסובים.

מַצָּה זוֹ שֶׁאָנוּ אוֹכְלִים, עַל שׁוּם מָה? עַל שׁוּם שֶׁלֹּא הִסְפִּיק בְּצֵקָם שֶׁל אֲבוֹתֵינוּ לְהַחֲמִיץ, עַד שֶׁנִּגְלָה עֲלֵיהֶם מֶלֶךְ מַלְכֵי הַמְּלָכִים, הַקָּדוֹשׁ בָּרוּךְ הוּא, וּגְאָלָם, שֶׁנֶּאֱמַר: וַיֹּאפוּ אֶת־הַבָּצֵק אֲשֶׁר הוֹצִיאוּ מִמִּצְרַיִם, עֻגֹת מַצּוֹת, כִּי לֹא חָמֵץ, כִּי גֹרְשׁוּ מִמִּצְרַיִם, וְלֹא יָכְלוּ לְהִתְמַהְמֵהַּ, וְגַם צֵדָה לֹא עָשׂוּ לָהֶם.

מגביהים את המרור ומראים למסובים.

מָרוֹר זֶה שֶׁאָנוּ אוֹכְלִים, עַל שׁוּם מָה? עַל שׁוּם שֶׁמֵּרְרוּ הַמִּצְרִים אֶת־חַיֵּי אֲבוֹתֵינוּ בְּמִצְרַיִם, שֶׁנֶּאֱמַר: וַיְמָרֲרוּ אֶת־חַיֵּיהֶם בַּעֲבֹדָה קָשָׁה, בְּחֹמֶר וּבִלְבֵנִים, וּבְכָל־עֲבֹדָה בַּשָּׂדֶה, אֶת כָּל־עֲבֹדָתָם, אֲשֶׁר עָבְדוּ בָהֶם בְּפָרֶךְ.

Beloved! It was He who knocked with is gavel on the podium.... If it had been some anonymous person who called the session of the United Nations to order, the State of Israel would never have come into being. But if the Beloved knocked on the chairman's podium, then the miracle occurred. 'Hark! My Beloved knocks!'" (*Kol Dodi Dofek*).

Maror zeh

The Haggadah says that we eat bitter herbs to remember how the Egyptians embit- tered the lives of our forefathers. But for the women, the bitterness of life does not express itself in back-breaking labor, in the travail of bricks and mortar, and in all man- ner of field work, no matter how physically challenging, painful, or grueling they may be. For a woman, the taste of maror evokes the bitterness experienced when her chil- dren are under siege, whether by Pharaoh of old or modern day enemies. When the safety and security of her family is at risk, when no matter what measures she takes, the bitter reality is that she cannot protect

The zero'a is not raised when saying the following:

Pesah, the Passover-lamb that our ancestors ate during the time of the *Bet Hamikdash*, was for what reason? It was because the Omnipresent passed over our ancestors' houses in Egypt, as it is said: "You shall say, It is a Passover-offering to the Lord, because He passed over the houses of the children of Israel in Egypt when He struck the Egyptians with a plague, and He saved our houses. And the people bowed and prostrated themselves."

The matzah is raised and shown.

This Matzah is eaten for what reason? It is because the dough of our ancestors did not have time to become leavened before the King of the kings of kings, the Holy One, blessed be He, revealed Himself to them and redeemed them. Thus it is said: "They baked Matzah-cakes from the dough that they had brought out of Egypt, because it was not leavened; for they had been driven out of Egypt and could not delay, and they had also not prepared any [other] provisions."

The maror is raised and shown.

This maror is eaten for what reason? It is because the Egyptians embittered our ancestors' lives in Egypt, as it is said: "They made their lives bitter with hard service, with mortar and with bricks, and with all manner of service in the field; all their service which they made them serve with rigor."

Prague Haggadah 1526

יֵשׁ מִנְהָג בָּעוֹלָם
שֶׁהָאִישׁ מוֹרֶה עַל
הָאִשָּׁה מִשּׁוּם שֶׁאָמַ
אִשָּׁה רָעָה מַר מִמָּוֶת.

her loved ones from sudden terror, murder, maiming, or mayhem. May this Passover bring us the blessed sweetness of a world at peace (Rookie Billet).

The Prague Haggadah of 1526, printed by Gershon Cohen and his associates, is one of the earliest printed haggadot with impressive woodcuts. Unfortunately, among the instructions in this Haggadah is the following: "There is a custom in the world to point to one's wife when saying '*maror zeh*, this bitterness,' as it says, 'a bad wife is more bitter than death.'" (Cf. Kohelet 7:26, "Now, I find women more bitter than

Washington Haggadah

בְּכָל־דּוֹר וָדוֹר חַיָּב אָדָם

לְהַרְאוֹת (מנהג ספרד) | לִרְאוֹת (מנהג אשכנז)

אֶת־עַצְמוֹ, כְּאִלּוּ הוּא יָצָא מִמִּצְרַיִם, שֶׁנֶּאֱמַר: וְהִגַּדְתָּ לְבִנְךָ בַּיּוֹם הַהוּא לֵאמֹר: בַּעֲבוּר זֶה עָשָׂה יְיָ לִי, בְּצֵאתִי מִמִּצְרָיִם. לֹא אֶת־אֲבוֹתֵינוּ בִּלְבָד, גָּאַל הַקָּדוֹשׁ בָּרוּךְ הוּא, אֶלָּא אַף אוֹתָנוּ גָּאַל עִמָּהֶם, שֶׁנֶּאֱמַר: וְאוֹתָנוּ הוֹצִיא מִשָּׁם, לְמַעַן הָבִיא אֹתָנוּ, לָתֶת לָנוּ אֶת־הָאָרֶץ אֲשֶׁר נִשְׁבַּע לַאֲבֹתֵינוּ.

מכסים את המצות ומגביהים את הכוס ואומרים:

לְפִיכָךְ אֲנַחְנוּ חַיָּבִים לְהוֹדוֹת, לְהַלֵּל, לְשַׁבֵּחַ, לְפָאֵר, לְרוֹמֵם, לְהַדֵּר, לְבָרֵךְ, לְעַלֵּה, וּלְקַלֵּס, לְמִי שֶׁעָשָׂה לַאֲבוֹתֵינוּ וְלָנוּ אֶת־כָּל־

---

death; she is all traps, her hands are fetters and her heart is snares. He who is pleasing to God escapes her, and who is displeasing is caught by her.") In the 15th-century German "Washington Haggadah," a man holding the maror is shown pointing to a woman who is holding a double-edged sword. (Cf. Proverbs 5:4, "but in the end she is as bitter as wormwood, sharp as a double-edged sword.") In the the Haggadah included in the Italian "Rothschild Miscellany" of the same period, a man holds the maror with one hand and touches his wife's forehead with the other. Of course, there is no such legitimate outrageous custom, but it is not the only instance of someone presenting distasteful "humor" as part of a "tradition."

Rothschild Miscellany

In every generation a person is obliged to regard himself as if he had gone out of Egypt
Nechama Leibowitz points out that this declaration has its roots in the *Mikra Bikkurim*, the declaration made when the first fruits are brought to the Temple: "I have come to the Land which the Lord swore to our fathers to give it to them" (*Deut.* 26:3). It is he who has come to the Land, not his ancestors. "Every generation had to regard itself brought to the Land by the Almighty. It had not to take the country for granted, as something bequeathed by its ancestors. Rather, the Israelites in every generation had to behave as if they themselves had just been brought there by the power and

In every generation a person is obligated to regard himself as if he had come out of Egypt, as it is said: "You shall tell your child on that day, it is because of this that the Lord did for me when I left Egypt." The Holy One, blessed be He, redeemed not only our ancestors from Egypt, but He redeemed also us with them, as it is said: "It was us that He brought out from there, so that He might bring us to give us the land that He swore to our ancestors."

The matzah is covered and the cup of wine raised.

Thus it is our duty to thank, to laud, to praise, to glorify, to exalt, to adore, to bless, to elevate and to honor the One who did all these

---

grace of their Creator. Every member of the House of Israel thus identifies himself personally with his people and its history, with what took place at the departure from Egypt, with being brought to the Holy land. He came to the Land; it was given to him" (*Studies in Devarim*).

Leaving *Mitzraim*

In every generation we must see ourselves as though we are leaving *Mitzrayim*. The Hebrew word for Egypt, *"Mitzrayim"* has been associated with *"mi'tzrim,"* which means "narrow straits." This sent me to the *Even Shushan* dictionary where I found the various meanings and uses of the word *"tzar."* As I read them with the eyes and ears of a Jerusalemite who has lived through several years of the intifada, each meaning resonated deep within me.

First, we find narrowness in its most physical sense, a space so limited one can turn neither to the right nor to the left – no room to move, as we say today. Next, we read about *"tzar ofek"* – horizons which are limited and minds which are narrow. Then there is *"lehem tzar,"* literally bread which is rationed – food that is less than one's minimal needs, that is, poverty.

We move on to *"tzar ayin,"* a description

of people so miserly, so envious, that they cannot bear to see good befall others – a kind of emotional impoverishment. Then we reach the expression *"b'tzar lo,"* someone in psychological distress –a people in their time of need. And then *"b'tzar ruho,"* an expression that describes those steeped in anxiety and suffering, whose soul is bitter – a kind of anguish or poverty of spirit.

Finally, and most to the point, there is the use of *"tzar"* to indicate an enemy, or one who hates you, as in *"ish tzar ve-oyev, Haman ha- ra hazeh"* and also in *"Avinu Malkeinu, kaleh kol tzar mastin mai'aleynu."*

As we sit here in Jerusalem, reliving our Exodus from Egypt, we pray to be lifted out of the dire straits we find ourselves in today, to a space of freedom and redemption (Ricki Bernstein).

To give us the land

When the daughters of Zelophehad (*Numbers* 27:1–12) heard that the land was being divided among men to the exclusion of women, they assembled together to take counsel. They said, "The compassion of God is not as the compassion of men. The compassion of men extends to men more than to women, but thus is not the com-

הַנִּסִּים הָאֵלּוּ. הוֹצִיאָנוּ מֵעַבְדוּת לְחֵרוּת, מִיָּגוֹן לְשִׂמְחָה, וּמֵאֵבֶל לְיוֹם טוֹב, וּמֵאֲפֵלָה לְאוֹר גָּדוֹל, וּמִשִּׁעְבּוּד לִגְאֻלָּה. וְנֹאמַר לְפָנָיו שִׁירָה חֲדָשָׁה. הַלְלוּיָהּ:

יֵשׁ מַנִּיחִים אֶת הַכּוֹס וּמַגְבִּיהִים אוֹתָהּ שׁוּב בְּבִרְכַּת "אֲשֶׁר גְּאָלָנוּ".

הַלְלוּיָהּ. הַלְלוּ עַבְדֵי יְיָ, הַלְלוּ אֶת־שֵׁם יְיָ: יְהִי שֵׁם יְיָ מְבֹרָךְ, מֵעַתָּה וְעַד עוֹלָם: מִמִּזְרַח שֶׁמֶשׁ עַד מְבוֹאוֹ, מְהֻלָּל שֵׁם יְיָ: רָם עַל־כָּל־גּוֹיִם יְיָ, עַל הַשָּׁמַיִם כְּבוֹדוֹ: מִי כַּיְיָ אֱלֹהֵינוּ, הַמַּגְבִּיהִי לָשָׁבֶת: הַמַּשְׁפִּילִי לִרְאוֹת, בַּשָּׁמַיִם וּבָאָרֶץ: מְקִימִי מֵעָפָר דָּל, מֵאַשְׁפֹּת יָרִים אֶבְיוֹן: לְהוֹשִׁיבִי עִם־נְדִיבִים, עִם נְדִיבֵי עַמּוֹ: מוֹשִׁיבִי עֲקֶרֶת הַבַּיִת, אֵם הַבָּנִים שְׂמֵחָה, הַלְלוּיָהּ:

בְּצֵאת יִשְׂרָאֵל מִמִּצְרָיִם, בֵּית יַעֲקֹב מֵעַם לֹעֵז: הָיְתָה יְהוּדָה לְקָדְשׁוֹ, יִשְׂרָאֵל מַמְשְׁלוֹתָיו: הַיָּם רָאָה וַיָּנֹס, הַיַּרְדֵּן יִסֹּב לְאָחוֹר: הֶהָרִים רָקְדוּ כְאֵילִים, גְּבָעוֹת כִּבְנֵי־צֹאן: מַה־לְּךָ הַיָּם כִּי תָנוּס, הַיַּרְדֵּן תִּסֹּב לְאָחוֹר: הֶהָרִים תִּרְקְדוּ כְאֵילִים, גְּבָעוֹת כִּבְנֵי־צֹאן: מִלִּפְנֵי אָדוֹן חוּלִי אָרֶץ, מִלִּפְנֵי אֱלוֹהַּ יַעֲקֹב: הַהֹפְכִי הַצּוּר אֲגַם־מָיִם, חַלָּמִישׁ לְמַעְיְנוֹ־מָיִם.

בָּרוּךְ אַתָּה יְיָ, אֱלֹהֵינוּ מֶלֶךְ הָעוֹלָם, אֲשֶׁר גְּאָלָנוּ וְגָאַל אֶת־אֲבוֹתֵינוּ מִמִּצְרַיִם, וְהִגִּיעָנוּ לַלַּיְלָה הַזֶּה, לֶאֱכָל־בּוֹ מַצָּה וּמָרוֹר.

---

passion of God; his compassion extends equally to men and women and to all, as it is written, "The Lord is good to all, and His mercies are over all his works' (*Psalms* 145:9)."

The daughters of Zelophehad said to Moses, "Give us a possession among our father's brethren" (*Numbers* 27:4). R. Natan said, "The strength of faith of the women was therefore finer than that of the men.

For the men had said, 'Let us give ourselves a captain, and let us return to Egypt' (*Numbers* 14:4)" (*Sifre, Pinhehas* 133).

Kli Yakar notes that God's command to appoint the spies to scout out the land was phrased '*Shelah lekha anashim* – send *as you think* men...' (*Numbers* 13:1). You, Moses, thought that the men had a great affection for the land. I am therefore sending men *as you think*. But in my opinion, continues

miracles for our ancestors and for us. He took us from slavery to freedom, from sorrow to joy, and from mourning to festivity, and from deep darkness to great light, and from bondage to redemption. Let us therefore recite before Him *Halleluyah*, Praise God!

Some lower the cup for the following two paragraphs and then raise it for the blessing:
Halleluyah – Praise God! Offer praise, you servants of the Lord; praise the Name of the Lord. May the Lord's Name be blessed from now and to all eternity. From the rising of the sun to its setting, the Lord's Name is praised. The Lord is high above all nations, His glory is over the heavens. Who is like the Lord, our God, who dwells on high yet looks down so low upon heaven and earth! He raises the poor from the dust, He lifts the needy from the dunghill, to seat them with nobles, with the nobles of His people. He restores the barren woman to the house, into a joyful mother of children. *Halleluyah* Praise God.

When Israel went out of Egypt, the House of Jacob from a people of a strange language, Judah became His holy one, Israel His dominion. The sea saw and fled, the Jordan turned backward. The mountains skipped like rams, the hills like young sheep. What is with you, O sea, that you flee; Jordan, that you turn backward? Mountains, why do you skip like rams; like young sheep? Tremble, you earth, before the Lord, before the God of Jacob, Who turns the rock into a pool of water, the flint-stone into a spring of water.

Blessed are You, Lord, our God, King of the universe, who has redeemed us and redeemed our ancestors from Egypt, and enabled us to reach this night to eat matzah and maror. So too, Lord, our God and

---

God, it would have been better to send women, who have a greater love for the land and would not have spoken ill of it (Commentary to *Numbers* 13:1).

Who turns the rock into a pool of water, the flint-stone into a spring of water
When the Jews in the desert complained that they were thirsty, God told Moses, "I will be standing there before you on the rock at Horeb. Strike the rock and water will issue from it, and the people will drink" (*Exodus* 17:6). This water-flowing rock stayed with the Jews throughout their journey in the desert and is called "Miriam's Well" (BT *Pesahim* 54a, *Rashi s.v. be'er*), as it was given to Israel in recognition of Miriam's Song (*Exodus* 15:20–21) at the Red Sea (*Midrash Tanhuma Bemidbar* 2).

כֵּן, יְיָ אֱלֹהֵינוּ וֵאלֹהֵי אֲבוֹתֵינוּ, יַגִּיעֵנוּ לְמוֹעֲדִים וְלִרְגָלִים אֲחֵרִים,
הַבָּאִים לִקְרָאתֵנוּ לְשָׁלוֹם. שְׂמֵחִים בְּבִנְיַן עִירֶךָ, וְשָׂשִׂים
בַּעֲבוֹדָתֶךָ, וְנֹאכַל שָׁם מִן הַזְּבָחִים וּמִן הַפְּסָחִים (במוצש"ק יש
אומרים: מִן הַפְּסָחִים וּמִן הַזְּבָחִים), אֲשֶׁר יַגִּיעַ דָּמָם עַל קִיר
מִזְבַּחֲךָ לְרָצוֹן, וְנוֹדֶה לְךָ שִׁיר חָדָשׁ, עַל גְּאֻלָּתֵנוּ וְעַל פְּדוּת
נַפְשֵׁנוּ. בָּרוּךְ אַתָּה יְיָ, גָּאַל יִשְׂרָאֵל:

מברכים בורא פרי הגפן ושותים בהסיבת שמאל.

בָּרוּךְ אַתָּה יְיָ, אֱלֹהֵינוּ מֶלֶךְ הָעוֹלָם, בּוֹרֵא פְּרִי הַגָּפֶן:

(מנהג ספרד לשתות בלי ברכה)

רָחְצָה

נוטלים ידים ומברכים:

בָּרוּךְ אַתָּה יְיָ, אֱלֹהֵינוּ מֶלֶךְ הָעוֹלָם, אֲשֶׁר קִדְּשָׁנוּ בְּמִצְוֹתָיו, וְצִוָּנוּ
עַל נְטִילַת יָדָיִם:

When Miriam died, the well was taken away (BT Ta'anit 9a), and the people were left without water (Numbers 20:1). Once again God gave the people water from a rock (Numbers 20:11).

"The connection between opposites is Miriam's gift to the people. For this problem of 'adjacency,' of what vulgarly be called 'mood swings,' will describe the history of the Israelites throughout the wilderness.

Transcendent vision, followed by drought and skepticism: this will become a pattern that Miriam's well, essential but almost totally effaced in the Torah text, quietly addresses" (Avivah Gottlieb Zornberg, *The Particulars of Rapture*).

Second cup
"I have already written that the head of the household should not pour the wine for

God of our ancestors, enable us to reach other holidays and festivals that will come to us in peace with happiness in the rebuilding of Your city, and with rejoicing in Your service [in the *Bet Hamikdash*]. Then we shall eat of the sacrifices and of the Passover-offerings [*on a Saturday night invert the order to "of the Passover-offerings and of the sacrifices"*] whose blood shall be sprinkled on the wall of Your altar for acceptance; and we shall thank You with a new song for our redemption and for the deliverance of our souls. Blessed are You, Lord, who redeemed Israel.

Sephardic custom is to drink the second cup without a blessing beforehand.
Ashkenazim say:

Blessed are You, Lord, our God, King of the universe, who creates the fruit of the vine.

Drink the wine while reclining on the left.

RAHTZAH

The hands are washed folowed by recital of the following blessing.

Blessed are You, Lord, our God, King of the universe, who has sanctified us with His commandments and commanded us concerning the washing of the hands.

---

himself, but rather should have someone pour it for him as a sign of freedom. But we are not careful about this, as it appears haughty to instruct one's wife to pour the wine for him, the husband being no better than she. Rather he should pour for himself" (*Rabbi Yehiel Mikhal Epstein, Arukh HaShulhan, Orah Hayim 473:6*). Of course, there is no reason why husband and wife cannot pour for each other.

Ashkenazim say a *berakha* before each of the four cups. Sephardim do not say a *berakha* before the second and fourth cup, as the *berakha* on the preceding cup applies to both.

Rah'tzah

The feminine form of the word "washing" (*rah'tzah*) is used here to allude to the fact that Moses was saved by a woman when Bitya "the daughter of Pharaoh went down to bathe (*lirhotz*) at the river" (*Exodus 2:5*) and rescued him (*Be'er Avraham, Amsterdam Haggadah*).

מוֹצִיא

מגביהים את שלוש המצות ומברכים ברכת "המוציא":

בָּרוּךְ אַתָּה יְיָ, אֱלֹהֵינוּ מֶלֶךְ הָעוֹלָם, הַמּוֹצִיא לֶחֶם מִן הָאָרֶץ:

מַצָּה

מניחים למצה התחתונה להשמט, ואוחזים רק את העליונה והאמצעית הפרוסה ומברכים "על אכילת מצה", ומכוונים לפטור בברכה זו גם את המצה שבכריכה ובאפיקומן.

בָּרוּךְ אַתָּה יְיָ, אֱלֹהֵינוּ מֶלֶךְ הָעוֹלָם, אֲשֶׁר קִדְּשָׁנוּ בְּמִצְוֹתָיו וְצִוָּנוּ עַל אֲכִילַת מַצָּה:

בוצעים לכל אחד מהמסובים כזית מהמצה העליונה וכזית מהפרוסה ואוכלים בהסיבת שמאל.

Matzah

Eating matzah at the *seder* is a time-bound mitzvah, a category of commandments from which women are usually exempt. However, as with the laws of Shabbat (where women are obligated in the time-bound mitzvot because they are obligated in the prohibitions of Shabbat), women are included in the requirement to eat matzah at the *seder* because they are included in the prohibition of eating *hametz* (BT *Pesahim* 43b; *Rambam, Hilkhot Hametz u-Matzah* 6:10). Since men and women share an equal obligation in this mitzvah, men can fulfill their obligation by answering Amen to the *berakhah* made by a woman.

In addition to fulfilling the specific requirement to eat matzah at the *seder,* the matzot fulfill the requirement of *lehem mishne,* the two loaves of bread that are required for Shabbat and holiday meals to commemorate the double portion of man-

na the Jews miraculously received before each Shabbat and holiday while in the desert. Authorities disagree as to why a woman shares equally with men in the obligation for *lehem mishneh;* it might be, for example, because women too participated in the miracle of the manna, or because *no* positive rabbinic *mitzvah* carries the exemption for women that time-bound Torah *mitzvot* do (*Sefer Hayashar – Responsa of Rabbeinu Tam,* section 70d). But all agree that women have an obligation equal to those of men on Shabbat and holidays (*Mishnah Berurah* 274 no. 1). Thus all present can fulfill their own obligation through the wife's *hamotzie,* and those families in which the husband says *Kiddush* each Friday night and the wife says *hamotzie* may continue their custom at the Passover *seder.*

The obligation for eating matzah has a minimum quantity – a *kezayit* – that is not required for *lehem mishne.* Since the leader's

MOTZI

The three matzot are raised and the following blessing said:

Blessed are You, Lord, our God, King of the universe, who brings forth bread from the earth.

MATZAH

The bottom matzah is put down and the following blessing recited over the broken matzah and the top one.

(One should have in mind that this blessing also applies to the korekh *which will be with the third* matzah *and the eating of the* Afikoman.*)*

Blessed are You, Lord, our God, King of the universe, who has sanctified us with His commandments and commanded us concerning the eating of Matzah.

Eat a kezayit *(the volume of one olive) of each of the two* matzot *while reclining on the left.*

---

matzot will not suffice to give everyone a *kezayit*, a small piece of his or her matzot is supplemented by extra matzah on the table. A number of possibilities therefore present themselves with regard to the two *berakhot*, as *hamotzie* should be said over the *lehem mishne*. All can simply answer Amen to the leader's two *berakhot* – or answer Amen to the leader's *hamotzie* and say *al akhilat matzah* themselves – and eat a *kezayit* of matzah along with a small piece of the leader's *lehem mishnhe*. Alternately, the others at the table can have their own *lehem mishne* and say their own two *berakhot*, there being no distinction here between the men and women at the table. A third option relies on the opinion that the *hamtozie* need not necessarily be said on one's own *lehem mishneh*, allowing all to say their own two *berakhot* on the extra

matzah and supplement it with a piece of the leader's *lehem mishneh*.

Al akhilat matzah

When the Jewish prisoners at the Bergen-Belsen concentration camp did not have matzah in 1944, the following prayer was composed: "Our Father in heaven, behold it is evident and known to Thee that it is our desire to do Thy will and to celebrate the festival of Passover by eating matzah and by observing the prohibition of leavened food. But our heart is pained the enslavement prevents us and we are in danger of our lives. Behold, we are prepared and ready to fulfill Thy commandment 'And you shall live by them and not die by them.' We therefore pray to Thee that Thou may keep us alive and preserve us and redeem us speedily so that we may observe Thy

מָרוֹר

נוטלים כזית מרור, טובלים בחרוסת ומנערים, ומכוונים בברכת
"על אכילת מרור" לפטור גם את המרור שבכריכה.

בָּרוּךְ אַתָּה יְיָ, אֱלֹהֵינוּ מֶלֶךְ הָעוֹלָם, אֲשֶׁר קִדְּשָׁנוּ בְּמִצְוֹתָיו וְצִוָּנוּ
עַל אֲכִילַת מָרוֹר:

ואוכלים בלי הסיבה.

כּוֹרֵךְ

נוטלים כזית מהמצה התחתונה וכזית מרור, ויש שנוהגים שלא
לטבלו, וכורכים יחד ואוכלים בהסיבה, ללא ברכה, ואומרים:

זֵכֶר לַמִּקְדָּשׁ כְּהִלֵּל: כֵּן עָשָׂה הִלֵּל בִּזְמַן שֶׁבֵּית הַמִּקְדָּשׁ הָיָה
קַיָּם. הָיָה כּוֹרֵךְ פֶּסַח מַצָּה וּמָרוֹר וְאוֹכֵל בְּיַחַד, לְקַיֵּם מַה
שֶׁנֶּאֱמַר: עַל־מַצּוֹת וּמְרוֹרִים יֹאכְלֻהוּ:

שֻׁלְחָן עוֹרֵךְ

אוכלים ושותים כברכת ה' אשר נתן, ויש נוהגים בתחילת הסעודה לאכול ביצה במי מלח.

statutes and serve Thee with a perfect heart. Amen" (*Language of Faith*).

Haroset

Two explanations are given for the significance of the *haroset*. Rabbi Yohanan says that it is *zekher letit*, in remembrance of the mortar used by the slaves to make their bricks. Rabbi Levi says that it is *zekher letappuah*, in commemoration of the apple trees under which the Jewish women of Egypt gave birth, their having gone without complaint to the fields to deliver in order to escape Pharaoh's decree that the new-born

MAROR

Take a kezayit *(the volume of one olive) of the maror and dip it into the* haroset.
*(One should have in mind that this blessing also applies
to the maror eaten with the* korekh.*)*

Blessed are You, Lord, our God, King of the universe, who has sanctified us with His commandments and commanded us concerning the eating of maror.

Eat the maror without reclining.

KOREKH

A kezayit *of the third matzah and a kezayit of the maror are
combined like a sandwich. Some do not dip it in the* haroset.

Thus did Hillel do at the time of the Temple: He would combine the Passover lamb, *matzah* and *maror* and eat them together, as it said: "They shall eat it with *matzah* and bitter herbs."

Eat the korekh while reclining on the left.

SHULHAN OREKH

*Eat a festive meal. It is permitted to drink wine between the second and third
cups. Many have the custom to begin the meal with eggs dipped in salt water.*

---

male babies be killed (*Pesahim* 116a (Rashi) and *bt Sota* 11b). Hence the custom of using apples in making the *haroset*.

The *haroset*, then, is a sign of our oppression and of the courage shown by the Jewish women in the face of that oppression. "The Exodus celebrates the movement from oppression/slavery/distance from God to redemption/freedom/closeness to God," writes Ruth S. Fagin. "The dual meaning of *haroset* reminds us that oppression and redemption are linked as surely as the physical and spiritual are connected in our own lives. It is up to us

צָפוּן

אחר הסעודה נוטלים לכל המסובים מהמצה שהוצפנה לאפיקומן,
ואוכלים בהסיבת שמאל. אחר אכילת האפיקומן אין לאכול.

יש מוסיפים:

זֵכֶר לְקָרְבַּן פֶּסַח הַנֶּאֱכָל עַל הַשֹּׂבָע:

בָּרֵךְ

מוזגים כוס שלישי ונוטלים מים אחרונים.

שִׁיר הַמַּעֲלוֹת, בְּשׁוּב יְיָ אֶת שִׁיבַת צִיּוֹן הָיִינוּ כְּחֹלְמִים: אָז יִמָּלֵא
שְׂחוֹק פִּינוּ וּלְשׁוֹנֵנוּ רִנָּה, אָז יֹאמְרוּ בַגּוֹיִם הִגְדִּיל יְיָ לַעֲשׂוֹת
עִם אֵלֶּה: הִגְדִּיל יְיָ לַעֲשׂוֹת עִמָּנוּ הָיִינוּ שְׂמֵחִים: שׁוּבָה יְיָ אֶת
שְׁבִיתֵנוּ כַּאֲפִיקִים בַּנֶּגֶב: הַזֹּרְעִים בְּדִמְעָה בְּרִנָּה יִקְצֹרוּ: הָלוֹךְ
יֵלֵךְ וּבָכֹה נֹשֵׂא מֶשֶׁךְ הַזָּרַע, בֹּא יָבֹא בְרִנָּה נֹשֵׂא אֲלֻמֹּתָיו:

ויש מוסיפים:

תְּהִלַּת יְיָ יְדַבֶּר־פִּי, וִיבָרֵךְ כָּל־בָּשָׂר שֵׁם קָדְשׁוֹ לְעוֹלָם וָעֶד:
וַאֲנַחְנוּ נְבָרֵךְ יָהּ מֵעַתָּה וְעַד־עוֹלָם הַלְלוּיָהּ: הוֹדוּ לַיְיָ כִּי־טוֹב כִּי
לְעוֹלָם חַסְדּוֹ: מִי יְמַלֵּל גְּבוּרוֹת יְיָ, יַשְׁמִיעַ כָּל־תְּהִלָּתוֹ:

---

to take the symbol of our oppression and
transform it into something redemptive"
(*Lifecycles: Talmud Torah*).

Afikoman
We use the *afikoman matzah*, which once
accompanied the Paschal sacrifice, to
represent the sacrifice itself. The laws of
the Paschal sacrifice reflect the same dual
symbolism of slavery and freedom that the

matzah does. It must be eaten when we are
already satiated and without breaking any
bones, as befits a royal dining style. Yet we
must hurry and eat it by midnight to recall
the haste with which we left Egypt when
we were slaves. Similarly, we bid farewell
to the *seder* night with our *afikoman* in a
royally recumbent manner, our lingering
memories of the *seder* are of both bondage
and freedom, inextricably bound together

TZAFUN

*After the meal, take the Afikoman and divide it among all the members
of the household. Eat it in the reclining position. One does not eat or
drink after the Afikoman, except for the required cups of wine.*

Some say:

In remembrance of the Pascal sacrifice which was eaten to satiety.

BAREKH

The third cup is decanted and mayim aharonim *poured over the hands.*

A Song of Ascents. When the Lord will return the exiles of Zion, we
will have been like dreamers. Then our mouth will be filled with laugh-
ter, and our tongue with joyous song. Then will they say among the
nations, "The Lord has done great things for these." The Lord has done
great things for us, we were joyful. Lord, return our exiles as streams
in the Negev. Those who sow in tears will reap with joyous song. He
goes along weeping, carrying the bag of seed; he will surely come [back]
with joyous song, carrying his sheaves.

Some add:

Now let my mouth declare the Lord's praise and let the whole human
race bless his Holy name for all time. As for us, we will bless the Lord
from now on and forever more: Praise the Lord! Give thanks to the
Lord for He is good, for His kindness is everlasting. Who can describe
the mighty deeds of the Lord, or utter all his praise?

---

with the time of our final redemption
(Shani Taragin, *A Celebration of the Haggadah*, The Women's Beit Midrash).

Mayim aharonim

Birkat haMazzon is preceded by "mayim
aharonim," a custom of ritually rinsing
one's hands. A Talmudic source (*TB Hulin*
105b) declares its purpose to wash away the

harmful *melah Sedomit* (Sodomite salt) before ending the meal. The danger of *melah
Sedomit* is no longer current, and, as Tosafot
(*TB Berakhot* 53b, s.v., *Veheyitem kedoshim*),
the *Tur* (*Orah Hayim* 181), and *Shulhan
Arukh* (*Orah Hayim* 181:10) note, many
people no longer end the meal by washing
their hands with *mayim aharonim*.

Quite naturally, there was never any ex-

כשמברכים בזימון מתחילים כאן:

המזמן אומר:

רַבּוֹתַי/גְּבִירוֹתַי/חֲבֵרַי נְבָרֵךְ!

המסובים עונים והמזמן חוזר אחריהם:

יְהִי שֵׁם יְיָ מְבֹרָךְ מֵעַתָּה וְעַד עוֹלָם.

המזמן אומר:

בִּרְשׁוּת בַּעַל הַבַּיִת/בַּעֲלַת הַבַּיִת/מָרָנָן/רַבָּנָן/רַבּוֹתַי/חֲבֵרַי,
נְבָרֵךְ (בעשרה אֱלֹהֵינוּ) שֶׁאָכַלְנוּ מִשֶּׁלּוֹ.

---

emption for women protecting themselves by washing off the *melah Sedomit*. The alternate source for *mayim aharonim* – that one must "be holy" and wash one's hands before reciting the *berakha* (*TB Berakhot* 53b; *Tur Shulhan Arukh Orah Hayim* 181) – similarly applies equally to men and women. Thus, for example, Rabbi Moshe Sternbukh, vice president of the "ultra-Orthodox" Eidah Hareidit, recently wrote: "I have found no basis for distinguishing between men and women [in this matter].... and it is obvious that [the obligation of *mayim aharonim*] applies to women as it does to men. Indeed, I have seen that among the most pious people women do so" (*Teshuvot veHanagot*, #174).

Zimmun

One of the formal ways of expressing the idea that those eating together have transcended their individual identities is the *zimmun*, the "call" to say *Birkat haMazzon*. "Three who ate as one," says the Mishnah, "are required [to say] the *zimmun*" (*Mishnah Berakhot* 7:1; *TB Berakhot* 45a). The Talmud (*TB Arakhin* 3a) remarks that "all [including women] are obligated in *zimmun*," quoting the *baraita*: "Women recite

the *zimmun* among themselves and slaves recite the *zimmun* among themselves. But if a group of women, slaves and minors want to recite the *zimmun*, they may not" (*TB Berakhot* 45b).

Bet Yosef (*Tur Shulhan Arukh* 199. *s.v. she-yesh mefarshim lekayem*) quotes Semag's interpretation that the Gemara in *Arakhin* refers to a case where the women ate with three or more men, while the Gemara in *Berakhot* discusses a situation where three or more women ate together without any men present. In the former case they are obligated to recite *Birkat haZimmun*, while in the latter case it is optional. This interpretation is codified as the *pesak* of the *Shulhan Arukh* (*Orah Hayim*, 199:7); however, the Vilna Gaon is among the later authorities who side with Rosh in obligating three women to say *Birkat haZimmun* even if they ate together without any men present (*ibid., Beurei HaGra*. This was anticipated by *Sefer haRokeah*, no. 333.).

The fact that many contemporary women may not regularly say the *zimmun* reflects not some ideal but rather an accommodation to an unfortunate situation. The *Mishnah Berurah* (*Shulhan Arukh Orah Hayim* 199, n. 16) suggests that the rabbis

When the zimmun *is said before Birkat HaMazzon, begin here.*

If a minyan is present, the phrase "our God" is added.

Gentlemen, ladies, my friends, let us say the blessing!

The others respond:

May the Name of the Lord be blessed from now and for ever.

The Leader repeats the response and continues:
Insert the appropriate phrases:

With the permission of my parents/the head(s) of the household/
my masters/my teachers/my friends,
let us bless [our God], He of whose bounty we have eaten.

---

exempted women from the obligation in *Birkat haZimmun* if fewer than three men ate with them simply because they felt that most women could not recite *Birkat ha-Zimmun* and hence it would be unfair to obligate them.

Whether or not three women are halakhically obligated to say the *zimmun*, there is no doubt that they may, should they wish. *Shulhan Arukh* (*Orah Hayim* 199:7) takes specific note of this as do contemporary halakhic guides for women (e.g., R. David Auerbach, Halikhot Beita 12:6; and R. Yitzhak Yaakov Fuchs, Halikhot Bat Yisrael 3:14). If three or more men were present, the women would have to defer to them in leading the *zimmun*; within halakhah, obligation takes precedence over volunteerism, and the three men are obligated. Rabbi Shelomo Zalman Auerbach notes that the presence of one or two men eating with three women presents no impediment to saying *Birkat haZimmun*; in such a case one of the women rather than one of the men should lead the *zimmun*, but the men should answer (*Halikhot Beita* 12:6, n. 14). All agree that ten women eating together would not add the word *"E-loheinu,"* as that requires a quorum of ten adult men.

Bereshut...

Many have the custom that the head of the household leads the *zimmun* at the seder. But generally, the custom is that the guest leads the *zimmun* so that *Birkat ha-Orei-ah* – "the guest's blessing" – for the hosts can be said. Since the hosts have the prerogative to select those who will bless them, specific permission must be attained from them. Originally, all those who eat would fulfill their own obligation to say *Birkat haMazzon* by listening to the *Birkat haMazzon* said by the person leading the *zimmun* and answering Amen. Hence the leader of the *zimmun* must ask permission of all the others to act on their behalf. It is customary to also recognize the presence of other significant people at the table by specifically singling them out. On Shabbat, Sephardim also "ask permission" from the Shabbat Queen.

Kos shel berakha

The Talmud (*TB Berakhot* 51b) relates that the person who leads the *zimmun* at a meal passes around the *"kos shel berakha"* (the cup of wine over which *Birkat haMazzon* is said) to the members of the household as a form of blessing. Once Ulla visited

המסובים עונים:

בָּרוּךְ (בעשרה אֱלֹהֵינוּ) שֶׁאָכַלְנוּ מִשֶּׁלּוֹ וּבְטוּבוֹ חָיִינוּ.

וחוזר המזמן:

בָּרוּךְ (בעשרה אֱלֹהֵינוּ) שֶׁאָכַלְנוּ מִשֶּׁלּוֹ וּבְטוּבוֹ חָיִינוּ.

יחיד אינו אומר:

בָּרוּךְ הוּא וּבָרוּךְ שְׁמוֹ.

כשאין זימון מתחילים כאן:

בָּרוּךְ אַתָּה יְיָ, אֱלֹהֵינוּ מֶלֶךְ הָעוֹלָם, הַזָּן אֶת הָעוֹלָם כֻּלּוֹ בְּטוּבוֹ בְּחֵן בְּחֶסֶד וּבְרַחֲמִים, הוּא נוֹתֵן לֶחֶם לְכָל בָּשָׂר, כִּי לְעוֹלָם חַסְדּוֹ. וּבְטוּבוֹ הַגָּדוֹל תָּמִיד לֹא חָסַר לָנוּ, וְאַל יֶחְסַר לָנוּ מָזוֹן לְעוֹלָם וָעֶד. בַּעֲבוּר שְׁמוֹ הַגָּדוֹל, כִּי הוּא אֵל זָן וּמְפַרְנֵס לַכֹּל, וּמֵטִיב לַכֹּל, וּמֵכִין מָזוֹן לְכָל בְּרִיּוֹתָיו אֲשֶׁר בָּרָא (כָּאָמוּר: פּוֹתֵחַ אֶת יָדֶךָ, וּמַשְׂבִּיעַ לְכָל חַי רָצוֹן). בָּרוּךְ אַתָּה יְיָ, הַזָּן אֶת הַכֹּל:

נוֹדֶה לְךָ יְיָ אֱלֹהֵינוּ עַל שֶׁהִנְחַלְתָּ לַאֲבוֹתֵינוּ, אֶרֶץ חֶמְדָּה טוֹבָה וּרְחָבָה, וְעַל שֶׁהוֹצֵאתָנוּ יְיָ אֱלֹהֵינוּ מֵאֶרֶץ מִצְרַיִם, וּפְדִיתָנוּ מִבֵּית עֲבָדִים, וְעַל בְּרִיתְךָ שֶׁחָתַמְתָּ בִּבְשָׂרֵנוּ, וְעַל תּוֹרָתְךָ שֶׁלִּמַּדְתָּנוּ, וְעַל חֻקֶּיךָ שֶׁהוֹדַעְתָּנוּ, וְעַל חַיִּים חֵן וָחֶסֶד שֶׁחוֹנַנְתָּנוּ, וְעַל אֲכִילַת מָזוֹן שָׁאַתָּה זָן וּמְפַרְנֵס אוֹתָנוּ תָּמִיד, בְּכָל יוֹם וּבְכָל עֵת וּבְכָל שָׁעָה:

וְעַל הַכֹּל יְיָ אֱלֹהֵינוּ אֲנַחְנוּ מוֹדִים לָךְ, וּמְבָרְכִים אוֹתָךְ, יִתְבָּרַךְ

---

the Babylonian Amora R. Nahman, who was married to Yalta, the daughter of the Rosh Galuta. After leading *Birkat haMazzon*, Ulla passed the "*kos shel berakhah*: to Rav Nahman, who asked him to send it to Yalta too. He demurred, quoting R. Yo-

hanan that the Torah says (*Deut* 7:13) God "will bless the issue of your womb," using the masculine form of "your" instead of the phrase "her womb," thereby indicating that progeny receives its blessing through the father and not the mother. There was

The others respond:

Blessed be [our God], He of whose bounty we have eaten.

The leader repeats this response and all continue.

(If the zimmun *is not said, all begin here.)*

Blessed are You, Lord, our God, King of the universe, who, in His goodness, feeds the whole world with grace, with kindness and with mercy. He gives food to all flesh, for His kindness is everlasting. Through His great goodness to us continuously we do not lack food, and may we never lack it, for the sake of His great Name. For He is a [benevolent] God who feeds and sustains all, does good to all, and prepares food for all His creatures whom He has created. (As it is said: You open Your hand and satisfy the desire of every living thing.) Blessed are You, Lord, who provides food for all.

We thank You, Lord, our God, for having given as a heritage to our ancestors a precious, good and spacious land; for having brought us out, Lord our God, from the land of Egypt and redeemed us from the house of slaves; for Your covenant which You have sealed in our flesh; for Your Torah which You have taught us; for Your statutes which You have made known to us; for the life, favor and kindness which You have graciously bestowed upon us; and for the food we eat with which You constantly feed and sustain us every day, at all times, and at every hour.

For all this, Lord our God, we thank You and bless You. May Your Name be blessed by the mouth of every living being, constantly and

---

therefore no need to extend the blessing to Yalta herself.

When Yalta heard the slight, she was enraged and went to the storage room and smashed four hundred jars of wine. Rav Nahman then asked Ulla to send her another cup of wine. He did, along with a message that all wine from that casket is of *berakhah*. She retorted, "Gossip comes from the people who wander around the cities [a reference to the fact that Ulla was known for traveling around the cities of Israel], and lice from the ragpickers."

Yalta's self-respect emerged not only from the family status, but from her understanding of halakhah. For example, she said: "For everything that the Torah has forbidden us, it has permitted us something in its place which is similar in kind. It is forbidden to eat blood, but it is permis-

שִׁמְךָ בְּפִי כָּל חַי תָּמִיד לְעוֹלָם וָעֶד. כַּכָּתוּב: וְאָכַלְתָּ וְשָׂבָעְתָּ, וּבֵרַכְתָּ אֶת יְיָ אֱלֹהֶיךָ עַל הָאָרֶץ הַטֹּבָה אֲשֶׁר נָתַן לָךְ. בָּרוּךְ אַתָּה יְיָ, עַל הָאָרֶץ וְעַל הַמָּזוֹן:

רַחֵם (נָא) יְיָ אֱלֹהֵינוּ, עַל יִשְׂרָאֵל עַמֶּךָ, וְעַל יְרוּשָׁלַיִם עִירֶךָ, וְעַל צִיּוֹן מִשְׁכַּן כְּבוֹדֶךָ, וְעַל מַלְכוּת בֵּית דָּוִד מְשִׁיחֶךָ, וְעַל הַבַּיִת הַגָּדוֹל וְהַקָּדוֹשׁ שֶׁנִּקְרָא שִׁמְךָ עָלָיו. אֱלֹהֵינוּ, אָבִינוּ, רְעֵנוּ, זוֹנֵנוּ, פַּרְנְסֵנוּ, וְכַלְכְּלֵנוּ, וְהַרְוִיחֵנוּ, וְהַרְוַח לָנוּ יְיָ אֱלֹהֵינוּ מְהֵרָה מִכָּל צָרוֹתֵינוּ. וְנָא אַל תַּצְרִיכֵנוּ יְיָ אֱלֹהֵינוּ, לֹא לִידֵי מַתְּנַת בָּשָׂר וָדָם, וְלֹא לִידֵי הַלְוָאָתָם. כִּי אִם לְיָדְךָ הַמְּלֵאָה, הַפְּתוּחָה, הַקְּדוֹשָׁה וְהָרְחָבָה, שֶׁלֹּא נֵבוֹשׁ וְלֹא נִכָּלֵם לְעוֹלָם וָעֶד:

(בשבת: רְצֵה וְהַחֲלִיצֵנוּ יְיָ אֱלֹהֵינוּ בְּמִצְוֹתֶיךָ, וּבְמִצְוַת יוֹם הַשְּׁבִיעִי הַשַּׁבָּת הַגָּדוֹל וְהַקָּדוֹשׁ הַזֶּה. כִּי יוֹם זֶה גָּדוֹל וְקָדוֹשׁ הוּא לְפָנֶיךָ, לִשְׁבָּת־בּוֹ וְלָנוּחַ בּוֹ בְּאַהֲבָה כְּמִצְוַת רְצוֹנֶךָ. וּבִרְצוֹנְךָ הָנִיחַ לָנוּ יְיָ אֱלֹהֵינוּ, שֶׁלֹּא תְהֵא צָרָה וְיָגוֹן וַאֲנָחָה בְּיוֹם מְנוּחָתֵנוּ. וְהַרְאֵנוּ יְיָ אֱלֹהֵינוּ בְּנֶחָמַת צִיּוֹן עִירֶךָ, וּבְבִנְיַן יְרוּשָׁלַיִם עִיר קָדְשֶׁךָ, כִּי אַתָּה הוּא בַּעַל הַיְשׁוּעוֹת וּבַעַל הַנֶּחָמוֹת:)

אֱלֹהֵינוּ וֵאלֹהֵי אֲבוֹתֵינוּ, יַעֲלֶה וְיָבֹא וְיַגִּיעַ, וְיֵרָאֶה, וְיֵרָצֶה, וְיִשָּׁמַע, וְיִפָּקֵד, וְיִזָּכֵר זִכְרוֹנֵנוּ וּפִקְדוֹנֵנוּ, וְזִכְרוֹן אֲבוֹתֵינוּ, וְזִכְרוֹן מָשִׁיחַ בֶּן דָּוִד עַבְדֶּךָ, וְזִכְרוֹן יְרוּשָׁלַיִם עִיר קָדְשֶׁךָ, וְזִכְרוֹן כָּל עַמְּךָ בֵּית יִשְׂרָאֵל לְפָנֶיךָ, לִפְלֵיטָה לְטוֹבָה לְחֵן וּלְחֶסֶד וּלְרַחֲמִים, לְחַיִּים וּלְשָׁלוֹם בְּיוֹם חַג הַמַּצּוֹת הַזֶּה. זָכְרֵנוּ יְיָ אֱלֹהֵינוּ בּוֹ לְטוֹבָה, וּפָקְדֵנוּ בוֹ לִבְרָכָה, וְהוֹשִׁיעֵנוּ בוֹ לְחַיִּים (טוֹבִים). וּבִדְבַר יְשׁוּעָה וְרַחֲמִים, חוּס וְחָנֵּנוּ, וְרַחֵם עָלֵינוּ וְהוֹשִׁיעֵנוּ, כִּי אֵלֶיךָ עֵינֵינוּ, כִּי אֵל מֶלֶךְ חַנּוּן וְרַחוּם אָתָּה:

forever. As it is written: When you have eaten and are satiated, you shall bless the Lord your God, for the good land which He has given you. Blessed are You, Lord, for the land and for the food.

Have mercy, Lord our God, upon Israel Your people, upon Jerusalem Your city, upon Zion the abode of Your glory, upon the kingship of the house of David Your anointed, and upon the great and holy House which is called by Your Name. Our God, our Father, our Shepherd, feed us, sustain us, nourish us and give us comfort; and speedily, Lord our God, grant us relief from all our afflictions. Lord, our God, please do not make us dependent upon the gifts of mortal men nor upon their loans, but only upon Your full, open, holy and generous hand, that we may not be shamed or disgraced forever and ever.

(*On Shabbat add the following paragraph:* May it please You, Lord, our God, to strengthen us through Your commandments, and through the precept of the Seventh Day, this great and holy Shabbat. For this day is great and holy before You, to refrain from work and to rest thereon with love, in accordance with the commandment of Your will. In Your will, Lord, our God, bestow upon us tranquility, that there shall be no trouble, sadness or grief on the day of our rest. Lord, our God, let us see the consolation of Zion Your city, and the rebuilding of Jerusalem Your holy city, for You are the Master of [all] salvations and the Master of consolations.)

Our God and God of our fathers, may there ascend, come and reach, be seen and accepted, heard, recalled and remembered before You, the remembrance and recollection of us, the remembrance of our fathers, the remembrance of Mashiah the son of David Your servant, the remembrance of Jerusalem Your holy city, and the remembrance of all Your people the House of Israel, for deliverance, well-being, grace, kindness, mercy, good life and peace, on this day of the Festival of Matzot, on this Festival of holy convocation. Remember us on this day, Lord, our God, for good; recollect us on this day for blessing; help us on this day for good life. With the promise of deliverance and compassion, spare us and be gracious to us; have mercy upon us and deliver us; for our eyes are directed to You, for You, God, are a gracious and merciful King.

Rebuild Jerusalem the holy city speedily in our days. Blessed are You, Lord, who in His mercy rebuilds Jerusalem. Amen.

Blessed are You, Lord, our God, King of the universe, benevolent God, our Father, our King, our Might, our Creator, our Redeemer, our Maker, our Holy One, the Holy One of Jacob, our Shepherd, the Shepherd of Israel, the King who is good and does good to all, each and every day. He has done good for us, He does good for us, and He will do good for us; He has bestowed, He bestows, and He will forever bestow upon us grace, kindness and mercy, relief, salvation and success, blessing and help, consolation, sustenance and nourishment, compassion, life, peace and all goodness; and may He never cause us to lack any good.

May the Merciful One reign over us forever and ever. May the Merciful One be blessed in heaven and on earth. May the Merciful One be praised for all generations, and be glorified in us forever and all eternity, and honored in us forever and ever. May the Merciful One sustain us with honor. May the Merciful One break the yoke of exile from our neck and may He lead us upright to our land. May the Merciful One send abundant blessing into this house and upon this table at which we have eaten. May the Merciful One send us Elijah the Prophet – may he be remembered for good – and may he bring us good tidings, salvation and consolation.

Add the appropriate phrases in the following paragraph:

May the Merciful One bless my father, my teacher; my mother, my teacher; the master(s) of this house; them, their household, their children, and all that is theirs; my husband; my wife; my children; us, and all that is ours. Just as He blessed our forefathers, Abraham, Isaac and Jacob, "in everything," "from everything," with "everything," so may He bless all of us together with a perfect blessing, and let us say, Amen.

ברכת אורח (מנהג ספרד):

הָרַחֲמָן הוּא יְבָרֵךְ אֶת הַשֻּׁלְחָן הַזֶּה שֶׁאָכַלְנוּ עָלָיו, וִיסַדֵּר בּוֹ כָּל מַעֲדַנֵּי עוֹלָם, וְיִהְיֶה כְּשֻׁלְחָנוֹ שֶׁל אַבְרָהָם אָבִינוּ, כָּל רָעֵב מִמֶּנּוּ יֹאכַל וְכָל צָמֵא מִמֶּנּוּ יִשְׁתֶּה, וְאַל יֶחְסַר מִמֶּנּוּ כָּל טוּב לָעַד וּלְעוֹלְמֵי עוֹלָמִים, אָמֵן. הָרַחֲמָן הוּא יְבָרֵךְ בַּעֲלֵי הַבַּיִת הַזֶּה וּבַעֲלֵי הַסְּעֻדָה הַזֹּאת, הֵם וּמִשְׁפַּחְתָּם וְכָל אֲשֶׁר לָהֶם, בְּבָנִים וּבָנוֹת שֶׁיִּחְיוּ וּבִנְכָסִים שֶׁיִּרְבּוּ. בָּרֵךְ יְיָ חֵילוֹ, וּפֹעַל יָדָיו תִּרְצֶה. וְיִהְיוּ נְכָסֵיהֶם וּנְכָסֵינוּ מֻצְלָחִים וּקְרוֹבִים לָעִיר, וְאַל יִזְדַּקְּקוּ לִפְנֵיהֶם וְלֹא לְפָנֵינוּ שׁוּם דְּבַר חֵטְא וְהִרְהוּר עָוֹן, שָׂשׂ וְשָׂמֵחַ כָּל הַיָּמִים, בְּעֹשֶׁר וְכָבוֹד מֵעַתָּה וְעַד עוֹלָם. לֹא יֵבוֹשׁוּ בָּעוֹלָם הַזֶּה וְלֹא יִכָּלְמוּ לָעוֹלָם הַבָּא, אָמֵן כֵּן יְהִי רָצוֹן.

הָרַחֲמָן, הוּא יְבָרֵךְ אֶת מְדִינַת יִשְׂרָאֵל, רֵאשִׁית צְמִיחַת גְּאֻלָּתֵנוּ.

הָרַחֲמָן, הוּא יְבָרֵךְ אֶת כָּל הָעוֹמְדִים עַל מִשְׁמַר אַרְצֵנוּ בְּכָל מָקוֹם שֶׁהֵם.

בַּמָּרוֹם יְלַמְּדוּ עֲלֵיהֶם וְעָלֵינוּ זְכוּת, שֶׁתְּהֵא לְמִשְׁמֶרֶת שָׁלוֹם, וְנִשָּׂא בְרָכָה מֵאֵת יְיָ וּצְדָקָה מֵאֱלֹהֵי יִשְׁעֵנוּ, וְנִמְצָא חֵן וְשֵׂכֶל טוֹב בְּעֵינֵי אֱלֹהִים וְאָדָם:

(בשבת: הָרַחֲמָן, הוּא יַנְחִילֵנוּ יוֹם שֶׁכֻּלּוֹ שַׁבָּת וּמְנוּחָה לְחַיֵּי הָעוֹלָמִים.)

הָרַחֲמָן, הוּא יַנְחִילֵנוּ יוֹם שֶׁכֻּלּוֹ טוֹב, יוֹם שֶׁכֻּלּוֹ אָרוּךְ, יוֹם שֶׁצַּדִּיקִים יוֹשְׁבִים וְעַטְרוֹתֵיהֶם בְּרָאשֵׁיהֶם וְנֶהֱנִים מִזִּיו הַשְּׁכִינָה, וִיהִי חֶלְקֵנוּ עִמָּהֶם:

הָרַחֲמָן, הוּא יְזַכֵּנוּ לִימוֹת הַמָּשִׁיחַ וּלְחַיֵּי הָעוֹלָם הַבָּא.

Sepharic custom is for guests to add the following paragraph:

May the Merciful One bless this table from which we have eaten, and set upon it all the delicacies of the world. May it be like the table of our father Abraham – all who are hungry may eat from it and all who are thirsty may drink from it. May nothing good ever be missing from it! Amen. May the Merciful One bless the heads of this household who have provided us with this meal – them and their families. May their children live and their possessions increase. May their business enterprises prosper and be close-by. May neither they nor we experience sin or the inclination to sin. May they rejoice all their lives with riches and honor. May they not be disgraced or put to shame in this world or the next. Amen.

May the Merciful One bless the State of Israel, the first flowering of our redemption.

May the Merciful One bless all who stand guard over our country wherever they may be.

From On High, may there be invoked upon him and upon us such merit which will bring a safeguarding of peace. May we receive blessing from the Lord and just kindness from the God of our salvation, and may we find grace and good understanding in the eyes of God and man.

(*On Shabbat add the following sentence:* May the Merciful One cause us to inherit that day which will be all Shabbat and rest for life everlasting.)

May the Merciful One cause us to inherit that day which is all good, that everlasting day when the just will sit with crowns on their heads, enjoying the reflection of God's majesty. And may our portion be with them.

May the Merciful One grant us the privilege of reaching the days of the Mashiah and the life of the World to Come.

מִגְּדוֹל יְשׁוּעוֹת מַלְכּוֹ, וְעֹשֶׂה חֶסֶד לִמְשִׁיחוֹ, לְדָוִד וּלְזַרְעוֹ עַד עוֹלָם: עֹשֶׂה שָׁלוֹם בִּמְרוֹמָיו, הוּא יַעֲשֶׂה שָׁלוֹם, עָלֵינוּ וְעַל כָּל יִשְׂרָאֵל, וְאִמְרוּ אָמֵן:

יְראוּ אֶת יְיָ קְדֹשָׁיו, כִּי אֵין מַחְסוֹר לִירֵאָיו: כְּפִירִים רָשׁוּ וְרָעֵבוּ, וְדֹרְשֵׁי יְיָ לֹא יַחְסְרוּ כָל טוֹב: הוֹדוּ לַיְיָ כִּי טוֹב, כִּי לְעוֹלָם חַסְדּוֹ: פּוֹתֵחַ אֶת יָדֶךָ, וּמַשְׂבִּיעַ לְכָל חַי רָצוֹן: בָּרוּךְ הַגֶּבֶר אֲשֶׁר יִבְטַח בַּיְיָ, וְהָיָה יְיָ מִבְטַחוֹ: נַעַר הָיִיתִי גַם זָקַנְתִּי וְלֹא רָאִיתִי צַדִּיק נֶעֱזָב, וְזַרְעוֹ מְבַקֶּשׁ לָחֶם: יְיָ עֹז לְעַמּוֹ יִתֵּן, יְיָ יְבָרֵךְ אֶת עַמּוֹ בַשָּׁלוֹם:

אשכנזים וספרדים מברכים על כוס שלישי:

בָּרוּךְ אַתָּה יְיָ, אֱלֹהֵינוּ מֶלֶךְ הָעוֹלָם, בּוֹרֵא פְּרִי הַגָּפֶן:

שׁוֹתִים בַּהֲסִיבַת שְׂמֹאל.

מוֹזְגִים כּוֹס רְבִיעִי וְכוֹס שֶׁל אֵלִיָּהוּ הַנָּבִיא, פּוֹתְחִים אֶת הַדֶּלֶת וְאוֹמְרִים:

שְׁפֹךְ חֲמָתְךָ אֶל־הַגּוֹיִם אֲשֶׁר לֹא יְדָעוּךָ, וְעַל־מַמְלָכוֹת אֲשֶׁר בְּשִׁמְךָ לֹא קָרָאוּ: כִּי אָכַל אֶת־יַעֲקֹב, וְאֶת־נָוֵהוּ הֵשַׁמּוּ: שְׁפָךְ־עֲלֵיהֶם זַעְמֶךָ, וַחֲרוֹן אַפְּךָ יַשִּׂיגֵם: תִּרְדֹּף בְּאַף וְתַשְׁמִידֵם, מִתַּחַת שְׁמֵי יְיָ:

יש נוהגים למזוג כוס רביעי אחר "שפוך חמתך".

---

sible to eat liver, which is all blood.... It is forbidden to eat a predatory animal, but it is permitted to eat the tongue of a fish. It is forbidden to take a man's wife, yet one is allowed to marry a divorced woman during her husband's lifetime. A brother's wife is forbidden, yet a *yevamah*, his sister-in-law, is allowed" (*TB Hulin* 109b).

Sheva Berakhot

During the first week of marriage, *sheva berakhot* are repeated after *Birkat haMazzon* at every meal attended by the bride and groom, provided there is present a *minyan* of ten adult men (and, at those times when it is required, *panim hadashot*, someone who had not previously been at a meal cel-

He is a tower of salvation to His king, and bestows kindness upon His anointed, to David and his descendants forever. He who makes peace in His heights, may He make peace for us and for all Israel; and say, Amen.

Fear the Lord, you His holy ones, for those who fear Him suffer no want. Young lions are in need and go hungry, but those who seek the Lord shall not lack any good. Give thanks to the Lord for He is good, for His kindness is everlasting. You open Your hand and satisfy the desire of every living thing. Blessed is the man who trusts in the Lord, and the Lord will be his trust.

Ashkenazim and Sephardim recite a blessing over the third cup.

Blessed are You, Lord, our God, King of the universe, who creates the fruit of the vine.

Drink the wine while reclining on the left.

The fourth cup is poured, as is Elijah's Cup. The door is opened and the following said:

Pour out Your wrath upon the nations that do not acknowledge You, and upon the kingdoms that do not call upon Your Name. For they have devoured Jacob and laid waste his habitation. Pour out Your indignation upon them, and let the wrath of Your anger overtake them. Pursue them with anger, and destroy them from beneath the heavens of the Lord.

Some people pour the fourth cup after saying "Pour out Your wrath."

---

ebrated by the couple). The *sheva berakhot* are distinct from *Birkat haMazzon*, which is said over a cup of wine, and for that reason a second cup of wine, over which the added blessings are said, is used. At the *seder*, however, this presents a technical problem, as one may not add an additional cup of wine after the third cup (which is the one over which each person says *Birkat haMazzon*). The solution, says R. Ovadiah Yosef (*Hazon Ovadia* 1:48), is to say *Birkat haMazzon* and the *sheva berakhot* over one cup of wine (and to say *borei pri hagafen*

as the first of the *sheva berakhot* instead of the last). This is the custom for *sheva berakhot* used by the Yemenite community throughout the year.

As to women saying one or more of the *sheva berakhot* at such meals, Rabbis Moshe Ehrenreich and Yosef Carmel, the *rashei kollel* of Jerusalem's *Makhon Eretz Hemda*, write that if the couple wants to honor a woman with saying one of the *berakhot*, "inasmuch as there is reason to permit it, it is not proper for those in attendance to create a conflict and thus prevent the

הַלֵּל

לֹא לָנוּ יְיָ, לֹא לָנוּ כִּי לְשִׁמְךָ תֵּן כָּבוֹד, עַל חַסְדְּךָ עַל אֲמִתֶּךָ: לָמָּה יֹאמְרוּ הַגּוֹיִם, אַיֵּה נָא אֱלֹהֵיהֶם: וֵאלֹהֵינוּ בַשָּׁמָיִם, כֹּל אֲשֶׁר חָפֵץ עָשָׂה: עֲצַבֵּיהֶם כֶּסֶף וְזָהָב, מַעֲשֵׂה יְדֵי אָדָם: פֶּה לָהֶם וְלֹא יְדַבֵּרוּ, עֵינַיִם לָהֶם וְלֹא יִרְאוּ: אָזְנַיִם לָהֶם וְלֹא יִשְׁמָעוּ, אַף לָהֶם וְלֹא יְרִיחוּן: יְדֵיהֶם וְלֹא יְמִישׁוּן, רַגְלֵיהֶם וְלֹא יְהַלֵּכוּ, לֹא יֶהְגּוּ בִּגְרוֹנָם: כְּמוֹהֶם יִהְיוּ עֹשֵׂיהֶם, כֹּל אֲשֶׁר בֹּטֵחַ בָּהֶם: יִשְׂרָאֵל בְּטַח בַּיְיָ, עֶזְרָם וּמָגִנָּם הוּא: בֵּית אַהֲרֹן בִּטְחוּ בַיְיָ, עֶזְרָם וּמָגִנָּם הוּא: יִרְאֵי יְיָ בִּטְחוּ בַיְיָ, עֶזְרָם וּמָגִנָּם הוּא:

יְיָ זְכָרָנוּ יְבָרֵךְ, יְבָרֵךְ אֶת בֵּית יִשְׂרָאֵל, יְבָרֵךְ אֶת בֵּית אַהֲרֹן: יְבָרֵךְ יִרְאֵי יְיָ, הַקְּטַנִּים עִם הַגְּדֹלִים: יֹסֵף יְיָ עֲלֵיכֶם, עֲלֵיכֶם וְעַל בְּנֵיכֶם: בְּרוּכִים אַתֶּם לַיְיָ, עֹשֵׂה שָׁמַיִם וָאָרֶץ: הַשָּׁמַיִם שָׁמַיִם לַיְיָ, וְהָאָרֶץ נָתַן לִבְנֵי אָדָם: לֹא הַמֵּתִים יְהַלְלוּ יָהּ, וְלֹא כָּל יֹרְדֵי דוּמָה: וַאֲנַחְנוּ נְבָרֵךְ יָהּ, מֵעַתָּה וְעַד עוֹלָם, הַלְלוּיָהּ:

אָהַבְתִּי כִּי יִשְׁמַע יְיָ, אֶת קוֹלִי תַּחֲנוּנָי: כִּי הִטָּה אָזְנוֹ לִי, וּבְיָמַי אֶקְרָא: אֲפָפוּנִי חֶבְלֵי מָוֶת, וּמְצָרֵי שְׁאוֹל מְצָאוּנִי, צָרָה וְיָגוֹן אֶמְצָא: וּבְשֵׁם יְיָ אֶקְרָא, אָנָּה יְיָ מַלְּטָה נַפְשִׁי: חַנּוּן יְיָ וְצַדִּיק, וֵאלֹהֵינוּ מְרַחֵם: שֹׁמֵר פְּתָאִים יְיָ, דַּלֹּתִי וְלִי יְהוֹשִׁיעַ: שׁוּבִי נַפְשִׁי לִמְנוּחָיְכִי, כִּי יְיָ גָּמַל עָלָיְכִי: כִּי חִלַּצְתָּ נַפְשִׁי מִמָּוֶת, אֶת עֵינִי מִן דִּמְעָה, אֶת רַגְלִי מִדֶּחִי: אֶתְהַלֵּךְ לִפְנֵי יְיָ, בְּאַרְצוֹת הַחַיִּים:

---

bride and groom from honoring those who bring them joy. This is especially true in our generation as it might offend the women who request, *leshem shamayim*, greater involvement in *avodat Hashem*, and one should attempt to respond positively to

their requests when the halakhah permits" (*Responsa be-Mareh ha-Bazak* 5:113).

Hallel

The Hallel of the *seder* night is unique. It is recited at night and not as part of the

HALLEL

Not to us, Lord, not to us, but to Your Name give glory, for the sake of Your kindness and Your truth. Why should the nations say, "Where, now, is their God?" Our God is in heaven, whatever He desires, He does. Their idols are of silver and gold, the product of human hands: they have a mouth, but cannot speak; they have eyes, but cannot see; they have ears, but cannot hear; they have a nose, but cannot smell; their hands cannot feel; their feet cannot walk; they can make no sound with their throat. Like them should be their makers, everyone that trusts in them. Israel, trust in the Lord! He is their help and their shield. House of Aaron, trust in the Lord! He is their help and their shield. You who fear the Lord, trust in the Lord! He is their help and their shield.

The Lord, mindful of us, will bless. He will bless the House of Israel; He will bless the House of Aaron; He will bless those who fear the Lord, the small with the great. May the Lord increase [blessing] upon you, upon you and upon your children. You are blessed unto the Lord, the Maker of heaven and earth. The heavens are the heavens of the Lord, but the earth He gave to the children of man. The dead do not praise God, nor do those that go down into the silence [of the grave]. But we will bless God, from now to eternity. *Halleluyah*, Praise God.

I love the Lord, because He hears my voice, my prayers. For He turned His ear to me; all my days I will call [upon Him]. The pangs of death encompassed me, and the agonies of the grave came upon me, trouble and sorrow I encounter and I call upon the Name of the Lord: Please, Lord, deliver my soul! The Lord is gracious and just, our God is compassionate. The Lord watches over the simpletons; I was brought low and He saved me. Return, my soul, to your rest, for the Lord has dealt kindly with you. For You have delivered my soul from death, my eyes from tears, my foot from stumbling. I will walk before the Lord in the

---

morning prayers; even though we end with a *berakhah*, we recite no *berakhah* here at the beginning; women are obligated even though it is a time-bound mitzvah; and it is recited seated rather than standing. If the *seder* has enabled us to see ourselves as

הֶאֱמַנְתִּי כִּי אֲדַבֵּר, אֲנִי עָנִיתִי מְאֹד: אֲנִי אָמַרְתִּי בְחָפְזִי, כָּל הָאָדָם כֹּזֵב:

מָה אָשִׁיב לַיְיָ, כָּל תַּגְמוּלוֹהִי עָלָי: כּוֹס יְשׁוּעוֹת אֶשָּׂא, וּבְשֵׁם יְיָ אֶקְרָא: נְדָרַי לַיְיָ אֲשַׁלֵּם, נֶגְדָה־נָּא לְכָל עַמּוֹ: יָקָר בְּעֵינֵי יְיָ, הַמָּוְתָה לַחֲסִידָיו: אָנָּה יְיָ כִּי אֲנִי עַבְדֶּךָ, אֲנִי עַבְדְּךָ בֶּן אֲמָתֶךָ, פִּתַּחְתָּ לְמוֹסֵרָי: לְךָ אֶזְבַּח זֶבַח תּוֹדָה, וּבְשֵׁם יְיָ אֶקְרָא: נְדָרַי לַיְיָ אֲשַׁלֵּם נֶגְדָה נָא לְכָל עַמּוֹ: בְּחַצְרוֹת בֵּית יְיָ, בְּתוֹכֵכִי יְרוּשָׁלַיִם, הַלְלוּיָהּ:

הַלְלוּ אֶת יְיָ, כָּל גּוֹיִם, שַׁבְּחוּהוּ כָּל הָאֻמִּים: כִּי גָבַר עָלֵינוּ חַסְדּוֹ, וֶאֱמֶת יְיָ לְעוֹלָם, הַלְלוּיָהּ:

הוֹדוּ לַיְיָ כִּי טוֹב,	כִּי לְעוֹלָם חַסְדּוֹ:
יֹאמַר נָא יִשְׂרָאֵל,	כִּי לְעוֹלָם חַסְדּוֹ:
יֹאמְרוּ נָא בֵית אַהֲרֹן,	כִּי לְעוֹלָם חַסְדּוֹ:
יֹאמְרוּ נָא יִרְאֵי יְיָ,	כִּי לְעוֹלָם חַסְדּוֹ:

מִן הַמֵּצַר קָרָאתִי יָּהּ, עָנָנִי בַמֶּרְחָב יָהּ: יְיָ לִי לֹא אִירָא, מַה יַּעֲשֶׂה לִי אָדָם: יְיָ לִי בְּעֹזְרָי, וַאֲנִי אֶרְאֶה בְשֹׂנְאָי: טוֹב לַחֲסוֹת בַּיְיָ, מִבְּטֹחַ בָּאָדָם: טוֹב לַחֲסוֹת בַּיְיָ, מִבְּטֹחַ בִּנְדִיבִים: כָּל גּוֹיִם סְבָבוּנִי, בְּשֵׁם יְיָ כִּי אֲמִילַם: סַבּוּנִי גַם סְבָבוּנִי, בְּשֵׁם יְיָ כִּי אֲמִילַם: סַבּוּנִי כִדְבֹרִים דֹּעֲכוּ כְּאֵשׁ קוֹצִים, בְּשֵׁם יְיָ כִּי אֲמִילַם: דַּחֹה דְחִיתַנִי לִנְפֹּל, וַיְיָ עֲזָרָנִי: עָזִּי וְזִמְרָת יָהּ, וַיְהִי לִי לִישׁוּעָה: קוֹל רִנָּה וִישׁוּעָה בְּאָהֳלֵי צַדִּיקִים, יְמִין יְיָ עֹשָׂה חָיִל: יְמִין יְיָ רוֹמֵמָה, יְמִין יְיָ עֹשָׂה חָיִל: לֹא אָמוּת כִּי אֶחְיֶה, וַאֲסַפֵּר מַעֲשֵׂי יָהּ: יַסֹּר יִסְּרַנִּי יָּהּ, וְלַמָּוֶת לֹא נְתָנָנִי: פִּתְחוּ לִי שַׁעֲרֵי צֶדֶק, אָבֹא בָם אוֹדֶה יָהּ: זֶה הַשַּׁעַר לַיְיָ, צַדִּיקִים יָבֹאוּ בוֹ: אוֹדְךָ כִּי עֲנִיתָנִי, וַתְּהִי לִי

lands of the living. I had faith even when I said, "I am greatly afflicted"; [even when] I said in my haste, "All men are deceitful."

What can I repay the Lord for all His kindness to me? I will raise the cup of salvation and call upon the Name of the Lord. I will pay my vows to the Lord in the presence of all His people. Precious in the eyes of the Lord is the death of His pious ones. I thank you, Lord, for I am Your servant. I am Your servant the son of Your handmaid, You have loosened my bonds. To You I will bring an offering of thanksgiving, and I will call upon the Name of the Lord. I will pay my vows to the Lord in the presence of all His people, in the courtyards of the House of the Lord, in the midst of Jerusalem. *Halleluyah*, Praise God.

Praise the Lord, all nations! Extol Him, all peoples! For His kindness was mighty over us, and the truth of the Lord is everlasting. *Halleluyah*, Praise God.

Give thanks to the Lord, for He is good, for His kindness is everlasting.
Let Israel say [it], for His kindness is everlasting.
Let the House of Aaron say [it], for His kindness is everlasting.
Let those who fear the Lord say [it], for His kindness is everlasting.

Out of narrow confines I called to God; God answered me with abounding relief. The Lord is with me, I will not fear; what can man do to me? The Lord is with me, through my helpers, and I can face my enemies. It is better to rely on the Lord than to trust in man. It is better to rely on the Lord than to trust in nobles. All nations surround me, but I cut them down in the Name of the Lord. They surrounded me, they encompassed me, but I cut them down in the Name of the Lord. They surrounded me like bees, yet they are extinguished like a fire of thorns; I cut them down in the Name of the Lord. You [my foes] pushed me again and again to fall, but the Lord helped me. God is my strength and song, and this has been my salvation. The sound of joyous song and salvation is in the tents of the righteous: "The right hand of the Lord performs deeds of valor. The right hand of the Lord is exalted; the right hand of the Lord performs deeds of valor!" I shall not die, but I shall live and relate the deeds of God. God has chastised

לִישׁוּעָה: אוֹדְךָ כִּי עֲנִיתָנִי, וַתְּהִי לִי לִישׁוּעָה: אֶבֶן מָאֲסוּ הַבּוֹנִים,
הָיְתָה לְרֹאשׁ פִּנָּה: אֶבֶן מָאֲסוּ הַבּוֹנִים, הָיְתָה לְרֹאשׁ פִּנָּה: מֵאֵת
יְיָ הָיְתָה זֹּאת, הִיא נִפְלָאת בְּעֵינֵינוּ: מֵאֵת יְיָ הָיְתָה זֹּאת, הִיא
נִפְלָאת בְּעֵינֵינוּ: זֶה הַיּוֹם עָשָׂה יְיָ, נָגִילָה וְנִשְׂמְחָה בוֹ: זֶה הַיּוֹם
עָשָׂה יְיָ, נָגִילָה וְנִשְׂמְחָה בוֹ:

| אָנָּא יְיָ הוֹשִׁיעָה נָּא: | אָנָּא יְיָ הוֹשִׁיעָה נָּא: |
| אָנָּא יְיָ הַצְלִיחָה נָּא: | אָנָּא יְיָ הַצְלִיחָה נָּא: |

בָּרוּךְ הַבָּא בְּשֵׁם יְיָ, בֵּרַכְנוּכֶם מִבֵּית יְיָ: בָּרוּךְ הַבָּא בְּשֵׁם יְיָ,
בֵּרַכְנוּכֶם מִבֵּית יְיָ: אֵל יְיָ וַיָּאֶר לָנוּ, אִסְרוּ חַג בַּעֲבֹתִים, עַד
קַרְנוֹת הַמִּזְבֵּחַ: אֵל יְיָ וַיָּאֶר לָנוּ, אִסְרוּ חַג בַּעֲבֹתִים, עַד קַרְנוֹת
הַמִּזְבֵּחַ: אֵלִי אַתָּה וְאוֹדֶךָּ, אֱלֹהַי אֲרוֹמְמֶךָּ: אֵלִי אַתָּה וְאוֹדֶךָּ,
אֱלֹהַי אֲרוֹמְמֶךָּ: הוֹדוּ לַיְיָ כִּי טוֹב, כִּי לְעוֹלָם חַסְדּוֹ: הוֹדוּ לַיְיָ כִּי
טוֹב, כִּי לְעוֹלָם חַסְדּוֹ:

מִנְהַג אַשְׁכְּנַז לוֹמַר "יְהַלְלוּךְ" כָּאן בְּלֹא חֲתִימַת בְּרָכָה,
וּמִנְהַג סְפָרַד לוֹמַר "יְהַלְלוּךְ" אַחֲרֵי "יִשְׁתַּבַּח"

יְהַלְלוּךְ יְיָ אֱלֹהֵינוּ (עַל) כָּל מַעֲשֶׂיךָ, וַחֲסִידֶיךָ צַדִּיקִים עוֹשֵׂי
רְצוֹנֶךָ, וְכָל עַמְּךָ בֵּית יִשְׂרָאֵל בְּרִנָּה יוֹדוּ וִיבָרְכוּ וִישַׁבְּחוּ וִיפָאֲרוּ
וִירוֹמְמוּ וְיַעֲרִיצוּ וְיַקְדִּישׁוּ וְיַמְלִיכוּ אֶת שִׁמְךָ מַלְכֵּנוּ, כִּי לְךָ טוֹב
לְהוֹדוֹת וּלְשִׁמְךָ נָאֶה לְזַמֵּר, כִּי מֵעוֹלָם וְעַד עוֹלָם אַתָּה אֵל.

---

if we ourselves had been freed from Egypt, we cannot help but burst forth into joyous praise and song. The song spills out spontaneously, whether it be night or day, whether we be seated or standing. Anyone who experiences the Redemption bursts into song and the category of time-bound commandments is irrelevant (Noa Jeselsohn, *A Celebration of the Haggadah*, The Women's Beit Midrash).

Hallel is recited at night here, the anniversary of the Exodus that turned our night into day, our darkness into light, our tragedy into happiness, our slavery into freedom (Jenifer Fishbein-Gold, *Yeshivat Ramaz Lekrat Shabbat Haggadah*).

me, but He did not give me over to death. Open for me the gates of righteousness; I will enter them and give thanks to God. This is the gate of the Lord, the righteous will enter it.

I thank You for You have answered me, and You have been a help to me. *(Repeat this verse.)*

The stone scorned by the builders has become the main cornerstone. *(Repeat this verse.)*

This was indeed from the Lord, it is wondrous in our eyes. *(Repeat this verse.)*

This day the Lord has made, let us be glad and rejoice on it. *(Repeat this verse.)*

O Lord, please help us! O Lord, please help us!

O Lord, please grant us success! O Lord, please grant us success!

Blessed is he who comes in the Name of the Lord; we bless you from the House of the Lord. *(Repeat this verse.)*

The Lord is Almighty, He gave us light; bind the festival-offering until [you bring it to] the horns of the altar. *(Repeat this verse.)*

You are my God and I will thank You; my God, I will exalt You. *(Repeat this verse.)*

Give thanks to the Lord, for He is good, for His kindness is everlasting. *(Repeat this verse.)*

The custom generally followed by Ashkenazim is to say the following paragraph here. Sephardim defer saying the paragraph until after Nishmat.

Lord, our God, all Your works shall praise You; Your pious ones, the righteous who do Your will, and all Your people, the House of Israel, with joyous song will thank and bless, laud and glorify, exalt and adore, sanctify and proclaim the sovereignty of Your Name, our King. For it is good to thank You, and befitting to sing to Your Name, for from the beginning to the end of the world You are Almighty God. Give thanks to the Lord, for He is good for His kindness is everlasting.

Birkat HaShir

"Wine is poured for the third cup of wine," says the Mishnah (*Pesahim* 10:7), "and Birkhat haMazzon is said over it. Then the fourth cup is poured, and over it we conclude the Hallel and recite *Birkat haShir*, 'the blessing of the song.'" The Gemara discusses the meaning of the term *Birkhat*

הוֹדוּ לַיְיָ כִּי טוֹב,												כִּי לְעוֹלָם חַסְדּוֹ:
הוֹדוּ לֵאלֹהֵי הָאֱלֹהִים,											כִּי לְעוֹלָם חַסְדּוֹ:
הוֹדוּ לַאֲדֹנֵי הָאֲדֹנִים,											כִּי לְעוֹלָם חַסְדּוֹ:
לְעֹשֵׂה נִפְלָאוֹת גְּדֹלוֹת לְבַדּוֹ,									כִּי לְעוֹלָם חַסְדּוֹ:
לְעֹשֵׂה הַשָּׁמַיִם בִּתְבוּנָה,										כִּי לְעוֹלָם חַסְדּוֹ:
לְרֹקַע הָאָרֶץ עַל הַמָּיִם,										כִּי לְעוֹלָם חַסְדּוֹ:
לְעֹשֵׂה אוֹרִים גְּדֹלִים,											כִּי לְעוֹלָם חַסְדּוֹ:
אֶת הַשֶּׁמֶשׁ לְמֶמְשֶׁלֶת בַּיּוֹם,									כִּי לְעוֹלָם חַסְדּוֹ:
אֶת הַיָּרֵחַ וְכוֹכָבִים לְמֶמְשְׁלוֹת בַּלָּיְלָה,							כִּי לְעוֹלָם חַסְדּוֹ:
לְמַכֵּה מִצְרַיִם בִּבְכוֹרֵיהֶם,										כִּי לְעוֹלָם חַסְדּוֹ:
וַיּוֹצֵא יִשְׂרָאֵל מִתּוֹכָם,										כִּי לְעוֹלָם חַסְדּוֹ:
בְּיָד חֲזָקָה וּבִזְרוֹעַ נְטוּיָה,										כִּי לְעוֹלָם חַסְדּוֹ:
לְגֹזֵר יַם סוּף לִגְזָרִים,											כִּי לְעוֹלָם חַסְדּוֹ:
וְהֶעֱבִיר יִשְׂרָאֵל בְּתוֹכוֹ,										כִּי לְעוֹלָם חַסְדּוֹ:
וְנִעֵר פַּרְעֹה וְחֵילוֹ בְיַם סוּף,									כִּי לְעוֹלָם חַסְדּוֹ:
לְמוֹלִיךְ עַמּוֹ בַּמִּדְבָּר,										כִּי לְעוֹלָם חַסְדּוֹ:
לְמַכֵּה מְלָכִים גְּדֹלִים,										כִּי לְעוֹלָם חַסְדּוֹ:
וַיַּהֲרֹג מְלָכִים אַדִּירִים,										כִּי לְעוֹלָם חַסְדּוֹ:
לְסִיחוֹן מֶלֶךְ הָאֱמֹרִי,										כִּי לְעוֹלָם חַסְדּוֹ:
וּלְעוֹג מֶלֶךְ הַבָּשָׁן,											כִּי לְעוֹלָם חַסְדּוֹ:
וְנָתַן אַרְצָם לְנַחֲלָה,											כִּי לְעוֹלָם חַסְדּוֹ:
נַחֲלָה לְיִשְׂרָאֵל עַבְדּוֹ,										כִּי לְעוֹלָם חַסְדּוֹ:
שֶׁבְּשִׁפְלֵנוּ זָכַר לָנוּ,											כִּי לְעוֹלָם חַסְדּוֹ:
וַיִּפְרְקֵנוּ מִצָּרֵינוּ,											כִּי לְעוֹלָם חַסְדּוֹ:
נוֹתֵן לֶחֶם לְכָל בָּשָׂר,										כִּי לְעוֹלָם חַסְדּוֹ:
הוֹדוּ לְאֵל הַשָּׁמָיִם,											כִּי לְעוֹלָם חַסְדּוֹ:

All continue:

Give thanks to the God of gods, for His kindness is everlasting;

Give thanks to the Lord of lords, for His kindness is everlasting;

Who alone does great wonders, for His kindness is everlasting;

Who made the heavens with understanding, for His kindness is everlasting;

Who stretched out the earth above the waters, for His kindness is everlasting;

Who made the great lights, for His kindness is everlasting;

The sun, to rule by day, for His kindness is everlasting;

The moon and stars, to rule by night, for His kindness is everlasting;

Who struck Egypt through their first-born, for His kindness is everlasting;

And brought Israel out of their midst, for His kindness is everlasting;

With a strong hand and with an outstretched arm, for His kindness is everlasting;

Who split the Sea of Reeds into sections, for His kindness is everlasting;

And led Israel through it, for His kindness is everlasting;

And cast Pharaoh and his army into the Sea of Reeds, for His kindness is everlasting;

Who led His people through the desert, for His kindness is everlasting;

Who struck great kings, for His kindness is everlasting;

And slew mighty kings, for His kindness is everlasting;

Sihon, king of the Amorites, for His kindness is everlasting;

And Og, king of Bashan, for His kindness is everlasting;

And gave their land as a heritage, for His kindness is everlasting;

A heritage to Israel His servant, for His kindness is everlasting;

Who remembered us in our lowliness, for His kindness is everlasting;

And delivered us from our oppressors, for His kindness is everlasting;

Who gives food to all flesh, for His kindness is everlasting;

Thank the God of heaven, for His kindness is everlasting.

נִשְׁמַת כָּל חַי תְּבָרֵךְ אֶת שִׁמְךָ יְיָ אֱלֹהֵינוּ, וְרוּחַ כָּל בָּשָׂר תְּפָאֵר וּתְרוֹמֵם זִכְרְךָ מַלְכֵּנוּ תָּמִיד. מִן הָעוֹלָם וְעַד הָעוֹלָם אַתָּה אֵל, וּמִבַּלְעָדֶיךָ אֵין לָנוּ מֶלֶךְ גּוֹאֵל וּמוֹשִׁיעַ, פּוֹדֶה וּמַצִּיל וּמְפַרְנֵס וּמְרַחֵם, בְּכָל עֵת צָרָה וְצוּקָה. אֵין לָנוּ מֶלֶךְ אֶלָּא אַתָּה: אֱלֹהֵי הָרִאשׁוֹנִים וְהָאַחֲרוֹנִים, אֱלוֹהַּ כָּל בְּרִיּוֹת, אֲדוֹן כָּל תּוֹלָדוֹת, הַמְהֻלָּל בְּרֹב הַתִּשְׁבָּחוֹת, הַמְנַהֵג עוֹלָמוֹ בְּחֶסֶד, וּבְרִיּוֹתָיו בְּרַחֲמִים. וַיְיָ לֹא יָנוּם וְלֹא יִישָׁן. הַמְעוֹרֵר יְשֵׁנִים וְהַמֵּקִיץ נִרְדָּמִים וְהַמֵּשִׂיחַ אִלְּמִים, וְהַמַּתִּיר אֲסוּרִים, וְהַסּוֹמֵךְ נוֹפְלִים, וְהַזּוֹקֵף כְּפוּפִים לְךָ לְבַדְּךָ אֲנַחְנוּ מוֹדִים.

אִלּוּ פִינוּ מָלֵא שִׁירָה כַיָּם, וּלְשׁוֹנֵנוּ רִנָּה כַּהֲמוֹן גַּלָּיו, וְשִׂפְתוֹתֵינוּ שֶׁבַח כְּמֶרְחֲבֵי רָקִיעַ, וְעֵינֵינוּ מְאִירוֹת כַּשֶּׁמֶשׁ וְכַיָּרֵחַ, וְיָדֵינוּ פְרוּשׂוֹת כְּנִשְׁרֵי שָׁמָיִם, וְרַגְלֵינוּ קַלּוֹת כָּאַיָּלוֹת, אֵין אֲנַחְנוּ מַסְפִּיקִים, לְהוֹדוֹת לְךָ יְיָ אֱלֹהֵינוּ וֵאלֹהֵי אֲבוֹתֵינוּ, וּלְבָרֵךְ אֶת שְׁמֶךָ עַל אַחַת מֵאֶלֶף אֶלֶף אַלְפֵי אֲלָפִים וְרִבֵּי רְבָבוֹת פְּעָמִים הַטּוֹבוֹת, שֶׁעָשִׂיתָ עִם אֲבוֹתֵינוּ וְעִמָּנוּ.

מִמִּצְרַיִם גְּאַלְתָּנוּ יְיָ אֱלֹהֵינוּ, וּמִבֵּית עֲבָדִים פְּדִיתָנוּ, בְּרָעָב זַנְתָּנוּ, וּבְשָׂבָע כִּלְכַּלְתָּנוּ, מֵחֶרֶב הִצַּלְתָּנוּ, וּמִדֶּבֶר מִלַּטְתָּנוּ, וּמֵחֳלָיִם רָעִים וְנֶאֱמָנִים דִּלִּיתָנוּ. עַד הֵנָּה עֲזָרוּנוּ רַחֲמֶיךָ, וְלֹא עֲזָבוּנוּ חֲסָדֶיךָ, וְאַל תִּטְּשֵׁנוּ יְיָ אֱלֹהֵינוּ לָנֶצַח. עַל כֵּן אֵבָרִים שֶׁפִּלַּגְתָּ בָּנוּ, וְרוּחַ וּנְשָׁמָה שֶׁנָּפַחְתָּ בְּאַפֵּינוּ, וְלָשׁוֹן אֲשֶׁר שַׂמְתָּ בְּפִינוּ, הֵן הֵם יוֹדוּ וִיבָרְכוּ וִישַׁבְּחוּ וִיפָאֲרוּ וִירוֹמְמוּ וְיַעֲרִיצוּ וְיַקְדִּישׁוּ וְיַמְלִיכוּ אֶת שִׁמְךָ מַלְכֵּנוּ. כִּי כָל פֶּה לְךָ יוֹדֶה, וְכָל לָשׁוֹן לְךָ תִשָּׁבַע וְכָל בֶּרֶךְ לְךָ תִכְרַע, וְכָל קוֹמָה לְפָנֶיךָ תִשְׁתַּחֲוֶה, וְכָל לְבָבוֹת יִירָאוּךָ, וְכָל קֶרֶב וּכְלָיוֹת יְזַמְּרוּ לִשְׁמֶךָ. כַּדָּבָר שֶׁכָּתוּב: כָּל עַצְמוֹתַי תֹּאמַרְנָה יְיָ מִי כָמוֹךָ. מַצִּיל עָנִי מֵחָזָק מִמֶּנּוּ, וְעָנִי וְאֶבְיוֹן מִגֹּזְלוֹ: מִי יִדְמֶה

The soul of every living being shall bless Your Name, Lord, our God; and the spirit of all flesh shall always glorify and exalt Your remembrance, our King. From the beginning to the end of the world You are Almighty God; and other than You we have no King, Redeemer and Savior who delivers, rescues, sustains, answers and is merciful in every time of trouble and distress; we have no King but You. [You are] the God of the first and of the last [generations], God of all creatures, Lord of all events, who is extolled with manifold praises, who directs His world with kindness and His creatures with compassion. Behold, the Lord neither slumbers nor sleeps. He arouses the sleepers and awakens the slumberous, gives speech to the mute, releases the bound, supports the falling and raises up those who are bowed.

To You alone we give thanks. Even if our mouths were filled with song as the sea, and our tongues with joyous singing like the multitudes of its waves, and our lips with praise like the expanse of the sky; and our eyes shining like the sun and the moon, and our hands spread out like the eagles of heaven, and our feet swift like deer we would still be unable to thank You Lord, our God and God of our fathers, and to bless Your Name, for even one of the thousands of millions, and myriads of myriads, of favors, miracles and wonders which You have done for us and for our ancestors before us. Lord, our God.

You have redeemed us from Egypt, You have freed us from the house of bondage, You have fed us in famine and nourished us in plenty; You have saved us from the sword and delivered us from pestilence, and raised us from evil and lasting maladies. Until now Your mercies have helped us, and Your kindnesses have not forsaken us; and do not abandon us, Lord our God, forever! Therefore, the limbs which You have arranged within us, and the spirit and soul which You have breathed into our nostrils, and the tongue which You have placed in our mouth they all shall thank, bless, praise, glorify, exalt, adore, sanctify and proclaim the sovereignty of Your Name, our King. For every mouth shall offer thanks to You, every tongue shall swear by You, every eye shall look to You, every knee shall bend to You, all who stand erect shall, bow down before You, all hearts shall fear You, and every innermost

לָךְ, וּמִי יִשְׁוֶה לָּךְ, וּמִי יַעֲרָךְ לָךְ: הָאֵל הַגָּדוֹל הַגִּבּוֹר וְהַנּוֹרָא, אֵל עֶלְיוֹן, קֹנֵה שָׁמַיִם וָאָרֶץ: נְהַלֶּלְךָ וּנְשַׁבֵּחֲךָ וּנְפָאֶרְךָ וּנְבָרֵךְ אֶת־שֵׁם קָדְשֶׁךָ. כָּאָמוּר: לְדָוִד, בָּרְכִי נַפְשִׁי אֶת יְיָ, וְכָל קְרָבַי אֶת שֵׁם קָדְשׁוֹ:

הָאֵל בְּתַעֲצֻמוֹת עֻזֶּךָ, הַגָּדוֹל בִּכְבוֹד שְׁמֶךָ, הַגִּבּוֹר לָנֶצַח וְהַנּוֹרָא בְּנוֹרְאוֹתֶיךָ, הַמֶּלֶךְ הַיּוֹשֵׁב עַל כִּסֵּא רָם וְנִשָּׂא:

שׁוֹכֵן עַד, מָרוֹם וְקָדוֹשׁ שְׁמוֹ. וְכָתוּב: רַנְּנוּ צַדִּיקִים בַּיְיָ, לַיְשָׁרִים נָאוָה תְהִלָּה.

מנהג ספרד		מנהג אשכנז	
בְּפִי	יְשָׁרִים תִּתְרוֹמָם.	בְּפִי	יְשָׁרִים תִּתְהַלָּל.
וּבְשִׂפְתֵי	צַדִּיקִים תִּתְבָּרַךְ.	וּבְדִבְרֵי	צַדִּיקִים תִּתְבָּרַךְ.
וּבִלְשׁוֹן	חֲסִידִים תִּתְקַדָּשׁ.	וּבִלְשׁוֹן	חֲסִידִים תִּתְרוֹמָם.
וּבְקֶרֶב	קְדוֹשִׁים תִּתְהַלָּל:	וּבְקֶרֶב	קְדוֹשִׁים תִּתְקַדָּשׁ:

וּבְמַקְהֲלוֹת רִבְבוֹת עַמְּךָ בֵּית יִשְׂרָאֵל, בְּרִנָּה יִתְפָּאַר שִׁמְךָ מַלְכֵּנוּ

---

haShir. Rabbi Yehuda says that it refers to the *Yehallelukhah* paragraph that normally concludes the Hallel. Rabbi Yohanan says that it is *Nishmat Kol Hai*, which normally concludes the *pesukei de-zimra* added to the morning service on Shabbat and holidays. This explains why various haggadot have conflicting texts at this point. The custom generally followed by Ashkenazim is to say the *Yehallelukhah* paragraph here without the concluding blessing. Sephardim defer saying the paragraph until after *Nishmat.*

The four cups of wine are generally taken to correspond to the four expressions of redemption in God's promise (*Exodus* 6:6–7): *ve-hotzeti* – I shall bring you forth;

ve-hitsalti – I shall save you; *ve-galati* – I shall redeem you; and *ve-lakakhti* – I shall take you to be My people. There is, however, a fifth expression of redemption, *ve-heveti* – I shall bring you to the land (v.8), which is taken by some to refer to a fifth cup of wine. Many explain Elijah's Cup (which is poured but not drunk) as this fifth cup which is set aside until Elijah will eventually settle the question. Maimonides refers to the fifth cup as permissible but not required (*Hilkhot Hametz u-Matzah* 8:10), as did many other authorities, including Rabbi Isaac Alfasi, Rashi (*Sefer HaPardes*), Rabbi Abraham ibn Daud, Rokeach, Rabbenu Nissim Gerondi, Rabbi Simeon ben Tzadok, and the Maharal of Prague (Rabbi

part shall sing praise to Your Name, as it is written: "All my bones will say, Lord, who is like You; You save the poor from one stronger than he, the poor and the needy from one who would rob him!" Who can be likened to You, who is equal to You, who can be compared to You, the great, mighty, awesome God, God most high, Possessor of heaven and earth! We will laud You, praise You and glorify You, and we will bless Your holy Name, as it is said: "[A Psalm] by David; bless the Lord, O my soul, and all that is within me [bless] His holy Name."

You are the Almighty God in the power of Your strength; the Great in the glory of Your Name; the Mighty forever, and the Awesome in Your awesome deeds; the King who sits upon a lofty and exalted throne.

He who dwells for eternity, lofty and holy is His Name. And it is written: "Sing joyously to the Lord, you righteous; it befits the upright to offer praise."

By the mouth of the upright You are exalted; by the lips of the righteous You are blessed; by the tongue of the pious You are sanctified; and among the holy ones You are praised.

In the assemblies of the myriads of Your people, the House of Israel, Your Name, our King, shall be glorified with song in every generation.

Menachem M. Kasher, *Haggadat Pesah Eretz-Yisraelit*).

Nechama Leibowitz explains that the fifth expression *"ve-heveti"* was not reflected in a cup of wine at the *seder* because, although the promise would be fulfilled, the Jews would subsequently go into exile. While the impact of the first four promises was eternal, the fulfillment of the fifth would be interrupted (*Studies in the Haggadah from the Teachings of Nechama Leibowitz*).

"And now, in our own time," writes Rabbi M. Kasher (*Haggadat Pesah Eretz-Yisraelit*), "when we have been privileged to behold the mercies of the Holy Name, blessed be He, and His salvation over us, in the establishment of the State of Israel, which

is the beginning of redemption [and fulfillment of *ve-heveti* – I will bring you to the land]...it is fitting and proper that we observe this pious act, the drinking of the fifth cup, as a form of thanksgiving."

Those who wish to follow this custom should conclude *Yehallelukha* with its normal blessing, *"Melekh mehulal batishbakot"* and then drink the fourth cup. (Ashkenazim say the *berakhah* beforehand while Sephardim omit it.) They should then fill the fifth cup – the officiant may use Elijah's Cup – and say over it *"Hodu,"* which is referred to as *"Hallel HaGadol* – the Great Hallel."

Be-fi Yisharim

The initial letter of the second word of

בְּכָל דּוֹר וָדוֹר. שֶׁכֵּן חוֹבַת כָּל הַיְצוּרִים, לְפָנֶיךָ יְיָ אֱלֹהֵינוּ, וֵאלֹהֵי אֲבוֹתֵינוּ, לְהוֹדוֹת לְהַלֵּל לְשַׁבֵּחַ, לְפָאֵר לְרוֹמֵם לְהַדֵּר, לְבָרֵךְ לְעַלֵּה וּלְקַלֵּס, עַל כָּל דִּבְרֵי שִׁירוֹת וְתִשְׁבָּחוֹת דָּוִד בֶּן יִשַׁי, עַבְדְּךָ מְשִׁיחֶךָ:

יִשְׁתַּבַּח שִׁמְךָ לָעַד מַלְכֵּנוּ, הָאֵל הַמֶּלֶךְ הַגָּדוֹל וְהַקָּדוֹשׁ בַּשָּׁמַיִם וּבָאָרֶץ, כִּי לְךָ נָאֶה, יְיָ אֱלֹהֵינוּ וֵאלֹהֵי אֲבוֹתֵינוּ, שִׁיר וּשְׁבָחָה, הַלֵּל וְזִמְרָה, עֹז וּמֶמְשָׁלָה, נֶצַח, גְּדֻלָּה וּגְבוּרָה, תְּהִלָּה וְתִפְאֶרֶת, קְדֻשָּׁה וּמַלְכוּת, בְּרָכוֹת וְהוֹדָאוֹת מֵעַתָּה וְעַד עוֹלָם.

אֵלּוּ שֶׁלֹּא אָמְרוּ "יְהַלְלוּךָ" לִפְנֵי "הַלֵּל הַגָּדוֹל," וְ"יִשְׁתַּבַּח" כִּדְלָעֵיל, אוֹמְרִים "יְהַלְלוּךָ" כָּאן:

אֵלּוּ שֶׁאָמְרוּ "יְהַלְלוּךָ" לִפְנֵי "הַלֵּל הַגָּדוֹל," אֵינָם חוֹזְרִים עָלֶיהָ אֶלָּא חוֹתְמִים "יִשְׁתַּבַּח" בִּבְרָכָה דִּלְהַלָּן:

יְהַלְלוּךָ יְיָ אֱלֹהֵינוּ כָּל מַעֲשֶׂיךָ, וַחֲסִידֶיךָ, וְצַדִּיקִים עוֹשֵׂי רְצוֹנֶךָ, וְעַמְּךָ בֵּית יִשְׂרָאֵל כֻּלָּם בְּרִנָּה יוֹדוּ, וִיבָרְכוּ וִישַׁבְּחוּ, וִיפָאֲרוּ אֶת שֵׁם כְּבוֹדֶךָ; כִּי לְךָ טוֹב לְהוֹדוֹת, וּלְשִׁמְךָ נָעִים לְזַמֵּר, וּמֵעוֹלָם וְעַד עוֹלָם אַתָּה אֵל. בָּרוּךְ אַתָּה יְיָ, מֶלֶךְ מְהֻלָּל בַּתִּשְׁבָּחוֹת. אָמֵן:

בָּרוּךְ אַתָּה יְיָ, אֶלְמֶלֶךְ גָּדוֹל בַּתִּשְׁבָּחוֹת, אֵל הַהוֹדָאוֹת, אֲדוֹן הַנִּפְלָאוֹת, הַבּוֹחֵר בְּשִׁירֵי זִמְרָה, מֶלֶךְ, אֵל, חֵי הָעוֹלָמִים:

בָּרוּךְ אַתָּה יְיָ, אֱלֹהֵינוּ מֶלֶךְ הָעוֹלָם, בּוֹרֵא פְּרִי הַגָּפֶן:

(מִנְהַג סְפָרַד לִשְׁתּוֹת בְּלִי בְרָכָה)

שׁוֹתִים בַּהֲסִבַּת שְׂמֹאל.

Concluding Birkat haShir
Those who have adopted the custom of drinking a fifth cup have already concluded Birkat haShir before Hodu. They drink the fifth cup here without a berakhah.

each line spells out Yitzhak in both the Ashkenazic and Sephardic version. The third letter of the third word in each line spells out Rivka in the Sephardic version.

For such is the obligation of all creatures before You, Lord, our God and God of our ancestors, to thank, to laud, to praise, to glorify, to exalt, to adore, to bless, to elevate and to honor You, even beyond all the words of songs and praises of David son of Yishai, Your anointed servant.

And therefore may Your Name be praised forever, our King, the great and holy God and King in heaven and on earth. For to You, Lord, our God and God of our ancestors, forever befits song and praise, laud and hymn, strength and dominion, victory, greatness and might, glory, splendor, holiness and sovereignty; blessings and thanksgivings to Your great and holy Name; from the beginning to the end of the world You are Almighty God.

Ashkenazim who have not already said the Yehallelulkha *paragraph above after Hallel conclude according to the Sephardic custom. Those who have already said the paragraph conclude:*	*Sephardic custom concludes with the following:*
Blessed are You, Lord, Almighty God, King, great and extolled in praises, God of thanksgivings, Lord of wonders, Creator of all souls, Master of all creatures, who takes pleasure in songs of praise; the only King, the Life of all worlds.	Lord, our God, all Your works shall praise You; Your pious ones, the righteous who do Your will, and all Your people, the House of Israel, with joyous song will thank and bless, laud and glorify, exalt and adore, sanctify and proclaim the sovereignty of Your Name, our King. For it is good to thank You, and befitting to sing to Your Name, for from the beginning to the end of the world You are Almighty God. Give thanks to the Lord, for He is good, for His kindness is everlasting. Blessed are You, Lord, King extolled in praises.

Sephardic custom is to drink the fourth cup without a blessing beforehand Ashkenazim say:

Blessed are You, Lord, our God, King of the universe, who creates the fruit of the vine.

Drink the wine while reclining on the left.

בָּרוּךְ אַתָּה יְיָ, אֱלֹהֵינוּ מֶלֶךְ הָעוֹלָם, עַל הַגֶּפֶן וְעַל פְּרִי הַגֶּפֶן, וְעַל
תְּנוּבַת הַשָּׂדֶה, וְעַל אֶרֶץ חֶמְדָּה טוֹבָה וּרְחָבָה, שֶׁרָצִיתָ וְהִנְחַלְתָּ
לַאֲבוֹתֵינוּ, לֶאֱכֹל מִפִּרְיָהּ וְלִשְׂבֹּעַ מִטּוּבָהּ. רַחֵם נָא יְיָ אֱלֹהֵינוּ עַל
יִשְׂרָאֵל עַמֶּךָ, וְעַל יְרוּשָׁלַיִם עִירֶךָ, וְעַל צִיּוֹן מִשְׁכַּן כְּבוֹדֶךָ, וְעַל
מִזְבְּחֶךָ וְעַל הֵיכָלֶךָ. וּבְנֵה יְרוּשָׁלַיִם עִיר הַקֹּדֶשׁ בִּמְהֵרָה בְיָמֵינוּ,
וְהַעֲלֵנוּ לְתוֹכָהּ, וְשַׂמְּחֵנוּ בְּבִנְיָנָהּ, וְנֹאכַל מִפִּרְיָהּ וְנִשְׂבַּע מִטּוּבָהּ,
וּנְבָרֶכְךָ עָלֶיהָ בִּקְדֻשָּׁה וּבְטָהֳרָה (בשבת: וּרְצֵה וְהַחֲלִיצֵנוּ בְּיוֹם
הַשַּׁבָּת הַזֶּה). וְשַׂמְּחֵנוּ בְּיוֹם חַג הַמַּצּוֹת הַזֶּה, כִּי אַתָּה יְיָ טוֹב
וּמֵטִיב לַכֹּל, וְנוֹדֶה־לְּךָ עַל הָאָרֶץ וְעַל פְּרִי גַפְנָהּ. בָּרוּךְ אַתָּה יְיָ,
עַל הָאָרֶץ וְעַל פְּרִי גַפְנָהּ: (על יין של חו״ל: פְּרִי הַגָּפֶן)

נִרְצָה

חֲסַל סִדּוּר פֶּסַח כְּהִלְכָתוֹ, כְּכָל מִשְׁפָּטוֹ וְחֻקָּתוֹ. כַּאֲשֶׁר זָכִינוּ
לְסַדֵּר אוֹתוֹ, כֵּן נִזְכֶּה לַעֲשׂוֹתוֹ. זָךְ שׁוֹכֵן מְעוֹנָה, קוֹמֵם קְהַל עֲדַת
מִי מָנָה. בְּקָרוֹב נַהֵל נִטְעֵי כַנָּה, פְּדוּיִם לְצִיּוֹן בְּרִנָּה.

לְשָׁנָה הַבָּאָה בִּירוּשָׁלַיִם הַבְּנוּיָה

Hasal Siddur Pesah
So many of the mitzvot of our *seder* are a
mere echo of something else. The shank-
bone is only a tiny remnant of the whole
lamb which should dominate our table;
the egg is in place of the poultry of the

Blessed are You, Lord our God, King of the universe, for the vine and the fruit of the vine, for the produce of the field, and for the precious, good and spacious land which You have favored to give as an heritage to our ancestors, to eat of its fruit and be satiated by its goodness. Have mercy, Lord our God, on Israel Your people, on Jerusalem Your city, on Zion the abode of Your glory, on Your altar and on Your Temple. Rebuild Jerusalem, the holy city, speedily in our days, and bring us up into it, and make us rejoice in it, and we will bless You in holiness and purity (*on Shabbat add:* May it please You to strengthen us on this Shabbat day) and remember us for good on this day of the Festival of Matzot. For You, Lord, are good and do good to all, and we thank You for the land and for the fruit of the vine. Blessed are You, Lord, for the land and for the fruit of her vine [*if the wine was from outside of Israel, conclude:* and for the fruit of the vine].

NIRTZAH

The order of the Pesah service is now completed in accordance with all its laws, ordinances and statutes. Just as we were worthy to perform it, so may we be worthy to do it in the future. O Pure One who dwells on high, raise up the congregation which is without number. Soon lead offshoots of the stock You have planted, redeemed to Zion, rejoicing in song.

NEXT YEAR IN REBUILT JERUSALEM!

festival sacrifice. *Korekh* is a reminder of how Hillel fulfilled the mitzvah of *korban pesah* when the Temple still stood and both matzah and maror have the status of Biblical commandments. The one mitzvah that would change everything, converting the *afikoman* from dessert to the main event of the evening, is the one mitzvah which we lack – the *korban pesah*. And so we turn to God and entreat Him to accept our *seder* in lieu of the sacrifice. But for once in our *seder*, this is *not* enough.

Broken and stricken by our exile from the Temple Mount, we beg *Hashem* that this be the final charade and that next year we may be able to take part in the actual event. We ask to be privileged to join the *aliyah la-regel* to the Temple, to offer our own *korban pesah*, and to sit with our *havurah* to eat the roasted lamb. "As we have merited to describe it, so may we merit to perform it! Next year in Jerusalem" (Sara Jo Ben Zvi, *A Celebration of the Haggadah, The Women's Beit Midrash*).

בחו"ל אומרים רק בלילה הראשון:

וּבְכֵן "וַיְהִי בַּחֲצִי הַלַּיְלָה"

אָז רֹב נִסִּים הִפְלֵאתָ בַּלַּיְלָה, בְּרֹאשׁ אַשְׁמוּרוֹת זֶה הַלַּיְלָה, גֵּר צֶדֶק נִצַּחְתּוֹ כְּנֶחֱלַק לוֹ לַיְלָה,

וַיְהִי בַּחֲצִי הַלַּיְלָה.

דַּנְתָּ מֶלֶךְ גְּרָר בַּחֲלוֹם הַלַּיְלָה, הִפְחַדְתָּ אֲרַמִּי בְּאֶמֶשׁ לַיְלָה, וַיָּשַׂר יִשְׂרָאֵל לְמַלְאָךְ וַיּוּכַל לוֹ לַיְלָה,

וַיְהִי בַּחֲצִי הַלַּיְלָה.

זֶרַע בְּכוֹרֵי פַתְרוֹס מָחַצְתָּ בַּחֲצִי הַלַּיְלָה, חֵילָם לֹא מָצְאוּ בְּקוּמָם בַּלַּיְלָה, טִיסַת נְגִיד חֲרֹשֶׁת סִלִּיתָ בְּכוֹכְבֵי לָיְלָה,

וַיְהִי בַּחֲצִי הַלַּיְלָה.

Va-Yehi ba-Hazi ha-Lailah

This *piyut* (liturgical hymn) refers to events that happened to various personalities at Passover time at various times in Jewish history. Yael Levine (*Midrashei Bitya bat Paroh*) identifies various events that occurred to female personalities on the first night of Pesah, and then, based on these sources, suggests two additional stanzas to the *piyyut*.

You have promised a covenant to the head of the *Imahot* at night (1). She who has been taken to Pharaoh and Avimelekh you have saved at night (2). She who has been likened to a rose suggested to exchange the blessings at night (3).

    It was in the middle of the night

The woman who gave birth cried and you smote the firstborn at night (4). You saved a firstborn, her candle did not extinguish at night (5). Hadassah was busy with the feast of Haman at night (6).

    It was in the middle of the night.

בְּרִית הִבְטַחְתָּ אֶת רֹאשׁ הָאִמָּהוֹת לָיְלָה. מוּבֶלֶת לְבֵית־פַּרְעֹה וְלַאֲבִימֶלֶךְ הִצַּלְתָּ לָיְלָה. מְשׁוּלַת שׁוֹשַׁנָּה יָעֲצָה לְהַחְלִיף הַבְּרָכוֹת בַּלַּיְלָה.

וַיְהִי בַּחֲצִי הַלַּיְלָה

צָעֲקָה הַיּוֹלֶדֶת וְהִכִּיתָ רֵאשִׁית אוֹנִים בַּלַּיְלָה. בְּכוֹרָהּ מִלַּטְתָּ, לֹא יִכְבֶּה נֵרָהּ בַּלַּיְלָה. הֲדַסָּה עֲסוּקָה הָיְתָה בִּסְעוּדָתוֹ שֶׁל הָמָן בַּלַּיְלָה.

וַיְהִי בַּחֲצִי הַלַּיְלָה

---

(1)   Sarah was also included in the "Covenant between the Pieces" (*Midrash Sekhel Tov*, ed. Buber, Genesis 15:18, p. 5). The Covenant with Abraham – and Sarah with him – was sealed on Passover night. Abraham is called *Rosh ha-Avot*, the Head of the Patriarchs (*Genesis Rabbah* 59,6), and the comparative term for Sarah is *Rosh ha-Imahot*.

THE FINAL SONGS

Outside of Israel, the following piyut *is recited only on the first night.*

VA-YEHI BE-HATZI HA-LAILAH

It came to pass, at midnight.

You made many miracles at night, at the beginning of the watches of this night. The righteous convert prevailed when he divided his company at night.

> It came to pass at midnight.

You judged the king of Gerar in a dream at night. The Armenian was struck with terror in the dark of the night. Israel strove with an angel and prevailed at night.

> It came to pass at midnight.

The first-born of the Egyptians were struck by You at midnight. They did not find their host when they arose at night. The army of the Prince of Haroshet You swept away with the stars of night.

> It came to pass at midnight.

---

(2) Sarah was taken to Pharaoh (*Genesis* 12) on this night (*Pirkei de-Rabbi Eliezer,* ed. Higger, chapter 26). She was taken by Avimelekh (*Genesis* 20) on this night as well (see the original *Va-Yehi ba-Hazi ha-Lailah piyut*).

(3) The exchange of the birthright between Jacob and Esau, initiated by Rebecca, took place on this evening (*Pirkei de-Rabbi Eliezer,* ed. Higger, chapter 31). Rebecca is compared to "a rose among the thorns" (*Shir ha-Shirim* 2:2) because she remained pure even though she grew up in a corrupt household (*Vayikra Rabbah* 23, 1).

(4) "Rachel, the granddaughter of Shuthelakh, was near childbirth, and with her husband she was treading the mortar, and the child was born and became entangled in the brick mold. Her cry ascended to the Throne of Glory, and that very night the angel Michael descended and took the brick mold with its clay before the Throne. The same night the Holy One, blessed be He, descended, and smote the firstborn of the Egyptians" (*Pirkei de-Rabbi Eliezer,* ed. Higger, chapter 47). The term *"reshit onim"* is based on the depiction of the Exodus in Psalms 78:51.

(5) Bitya, daughter of Pharaoh, saved Moses by night, and she herself, who was a firstborn, was saved from the plague of the firstborn (*Exodus Rabbah* 18.3).

(6) Hadassah, i.e., Esther, was busy with the feast of Haman at night (*Midrash Panim Aherim,* ed. Buber, p. 74).

יַעַץ מְחָרֵף לְנוֹפֵף אִוּוּי, הוֹבַשְׁתָּ פְגָרָיו בַּלַּיְלָה, כָּרַע בֵּל וּמַצָּבוֹ
בְּאִישׁוֹן לַיְלָה, לְאִישׁ חֲמוּדוֹת נִגְלָה רָז חֲזוֹת לַיְלָה,
וַיְהִי בַּחֲצִי הַלַּיְלָה.

מִשְׁתַּכֵּר בִּכְלֵי קֹדֶשׁ נֶהֱרַג בּוֹ בַּלַּיְלָה, נוֹשַׁע מִבּוֹר אֲרָיוֹת פּוֹתֵר
בְּעֲתוּתֵי לַיְלָה, שִׂנְאָה נָטַר אֲגָגִי וְכָתַב סְפָרִים בַּלַּיְלָה,
וַיְהִי בַּחֲצִי הַלַּיְלָה.

עוֹרַרְתָּ נִצְחֲךָ עָלָיו בְּנֶדֶד שְׁנַת לַיְלָה, פּוּרָה תִדְרוֹךְ לְשׁוֹמֵר מַה
מִּלַּיְלָה, צָרַח כַּשֹּׁמֵר וְשָׂח אָתָא בֹקֶר וְגַם לַיְלָה,
וַיְהִי בַּחֲצִי הַלַּיְלָה.

קָרֵב יוֹם אֲשֶׁר הוּא לֹא יוֹם וְלֹא לַיְלָה, רָם הוֹדַע כִּי לְךָ הַיּוֹם אַף
לְךָ הַלַּיְלָה, שׁוֹמְרִים הַפְקֵד לְעִירְךָ כָּל הַיּוֹם וְכָל הַלַּיְלָה, תָּאִיר
כְּאוֹר יוֹם חֶשְׁכַּת לַיְלָה,

וַיְהִי בַּחֲצִי הַלַּיְלָה:

בחו"ל אומרים רק בלילה השני:

וּבְכֵן "וַאֲמַרְתֶּם זֶבַח פֶּסַח"

אֹמֶץ גְּבוּרוֹתֶיךָ הִפְלֵאתָ בַּפֶּסַח, בְּרֹאשׁ כָּל מוֹעֲדוֹת נִשֵּׂאתָ פֶּסַח,
גִּלִּיתָ לְאֶזְרָחִי חֲצוֹת לֵיל פֶּסַח,
וַאֲמַרְתֶּם זֶבַח פֶּסַח.

דְּלָתָיו דָּפַקְתָּ כְּחֹם הַיּוֹם בַּפֶּסַח, הִסְעִיד נוֹצְצִים עֻגוֹת מַצּוֹת
בַּפֶּסַח, וְאֶל הַבָּקָר רָץ זֵכֶר לְשׁוֹר עֵרֶךְ פֶּסַח,
וַאֲמַרְתֶּם זֶבַח פֶּסַח.

The blasphemer planned to raise his hand against Jerusalem, and you defeated him by night. The idol Bel and its pedestal were overthrown in the darkness of the night. To the much beloved was the secret vision revealed at night.

It came to pass at midnight.

He who caroused from the holy vessels was slain that same night. He who was rescued from the lion's den interpreted the awesome dreams of night. The Agagite who cherished hatred wrote letters at night.

It came to pass at midnight.

You roused Your power against him when sleep fled at night. You will tread the winepress for he who asks, Watchman, what of the night. He shall answer like a watchman and say, The morning will come after this night.

It came to pass at midnight.

Bring near the day which is neither day nor night! Make known, Most High, that Yours is the day as well as the night. Appoint watchmen to Your city by day and night. Make shine as with the light of the day the darkness of the night.

It came to pass at midnight.

Outside of Israel, the following is recited only on the second night.
And you shall say, It is the sacrifice of Pesah.

You showed Your power on Pesah. You made our first festival Pesah. You revealed to the Ezrehite [Abraham] the wondrous midnight of Pesah.

And you shall say, It is the sacrifice of Pesah.

You knocked at his door in the midday heat on Pesah. He fed the angels unleavened cakes on Pesah. He ran to the herd – a memorial of the sacrifice of Pesah.

And you shall say, It is the sacrifice of Pesah.

זֹעֲמוּ סְדוֹמִים וְלֹהֲטוּ בָּאֵשׁ בְּפֶסַח, חֻלַּץ לוֹט מֵהֶם, וּמַצּוֹת אָפָה בְּקֵץ פֶּסַח, טִאטֵאתָ אַדְמַת מֹף וְנֹף בְּעָבְרְךָ בְּפֶסַח,
וַאֲמַרְתֶּם זֶבַח פֶּסַח.

יָהּ, רֹאשׁ כָּל אוֹן מָחַצְתָּ בְּלֵיל שִׁמּוּר פֶּסַח, כַּבִּיר, עַל בֵּן בְּכוֹר פָּסַחְתָּ בְּדַם פֶּסַח, לְבִלְתִּי תֵּת מַשְׁחִית לָבֹא בִּפְתָחַי בַּפֶּסַח,
וַאֲמַרְתֶּם זֶבַח פֶּסַח.

מְסֻגֶּרֶת סֻגָּרָה בְּעִתּוֹתֵי פֶסַח, נִשְׁמְדָה מִדְיָן בִּצְלִיל שְׂעוֹרֵי עֹמֶר פֶּסַח, שֹׂרְפוּ מִשְׁמַנֵּי פּוּל וְלוּד בִּיקַד יְקוֹד פֶּסַח,
וַאֲמַרְתֶּם זֶבַח פֶּסַח.

עוֹד הַיּוֹם בְּנֹב לַעֲמֹד, עַד גָּעָה עוֹנַת פֶּסַח, פַּס יָד כָּתְבָה לְקַעֲקֵעַ צוּל בְּפֶסַח, צָפֹה הַצָּפִית עָרוֹךְ הַשֻּׁלְחָן בַּפֶּסַח,
וַאֲמַרְתֶּם זֶבַח פֶּסַח.

קָהָל כִּנְּסָה הֲדַסָּה צוֹם לְשַׁלֵּשׁ בַּפֶּסַח, רֹאשׁ מִבֵּית רָשָׁע מָחַצְתָּ בְּעֵץ חֲמִשִּׁים בַּפֶּסַח, שְׁתֵּי אֵלֶּה רֶגַע, תָּבִיא לְעוּצִית בַּפֶּסַח, תָּעֹז יָדְךָ וְתָרוּם יְמִינֶךָ, כְּלֵיל הִתְקַדֶּשׁ חַג פֶּסַח,
וַאֲמַרְתֶּם זֶבַח פֶּסַח.

כִּי לוֹ נָאֶה, כִּי לוֹ יָאֶה

אַדִּיר בִּמְלוּכָה, בָּחוּר כַּהֲלָכָה, גְּדוּדָיו יֹאמְרוּ לוֹ: לְךָ וּלְךָ, לְךָ כִּי לְךָ, לְךָ אַף לְךָ, לְךָ יְיָ הַמַּמְלָכָה. כִּי לוֹ נָאֶה, כִּי לוֹ יָאֶה.

Ki Lo Na'eh
The Sefat Emet states: "Our Sages call Passover night *'seder'* (order) and say, 'the *siddur* (ordering) of Passover is accomplished.'"

This alludes to the fact that there is a natural order, a certain order for miracles and wonders. Thus we have the mitzvot of matzot and maror, since one is to give praise

The Sodomites angered God and were consumed with fire on Pesah. Lot, saved from them, baked unleavened cakes at the end of Pesah. You swept clean the land of Moph and Noph when You passed through on Pesah.

> And you shall say, It is the sacrifice of Pesah.

God, You destroyed the first-born on the night of Pesah. Master, You spared Your first-born because of the blood of the sacrifice of Pesah. You did not let the destoyer enter my doors on Pesah.

> And you shall say, It is the sacrifice of Pesah.

The beleagured city was besieged on Pesah. Midian was destroyed by a barley cake, the offering on Pesah. The Princes of Pul and Lud were consumed in a great fire on Pesah.

> And you shall say, It is the sacrifice of Pesah.

He was to be that day in Nob towards Pesah. The hand wrote prophesying the destruction of Zul on Pesah. "The watch was set, the table spread" on Pesah.

> And you shall say, It is the sacrifice of Pesah.

Hadassah assembled the people for a three-day fast on Pesah. The chief of an evil house you did hang on a fifty-cubit gallows on Pesah. "Both of these" will You bring in one moment on Utz on Pesah. Your hand will be strong, Your right hand uplifted as on the night you sanctified Pesah.

> And you shall say, It is the sacrifice of Pesah.

Outside of Israel, all of the following are recited on both nights:

KI LO NA'EH

Powerful in kingship, truly chosen, His troops sing to Him: "Yours, only Yours, O Lord, is the Majestic Kingdom." Beautiful praises are His due.

---

for the exile as well as for the redemption." Since we want to be included among those generations who are worthy of the *seder* of salvation, we try to behave in the manner of those who went out in the exodus from Egypt, in the fervent hope that we, too, will merit redemption. In each refrain, the work *lekha* appears seven times. The

דָּגוּל בִּמְלוּכָה, הָדוּר כַּהֲלָכָה, וָתִיקָיו יֹאמְרוּ לוֹ: לְךָ וּלְךָ, לְךָ כִּי לְךָ, לְךָ אַף לְךָ, לְךָ יְיָ הַמַּמְלָכָה. כִּי לוֹ נָאֶה, כִּי לוֹ יָאֶה.

זַכַּאי בִּמְלוּכָה, חָסִין כַּהֲלָכָה, טַפְסְרָיו יֹאמְרוּ לוֹ: לְךָ וּלְךָ, לְךָ כִּי לְךָ, לְךָ אַף לְךָ, לְךָ יְיָ הַמַּמְלָכָה. כִּי לוֹ נָאֶה, כִּי לוֹ יָאֶה.

יָחִיד בִּמְלוּכָה, כַּבִּיר כַּהֲלָכָה, לִמּוּדָיו יֹאמְרוּ לוֹ: לְךָ וּלְךָ, לְךָ כִּי לְךָ, לְךָ אַף לְךָ, לְךָ יְיָ הַמַּמְלָכָה. כִּי לוֹ נָאֶה, כִּי לוֹ יָאֶה.

מוֹשֵׁל בִּמְלוּכָה, נוֹרָא כַּהֲלָכָה, סְבִיבָיו יֹאמְרוּ לוֹ: לְךָ וּלְךָ, לְךָ כִּי לְךָ, לְךָ אַף לְךָ, לְךָ יְיָ הַמַּמְלָכָה. כִּי לוֹ נָאֶה, כִּי לוֹ יָאֶה.

עָנָיו בִּמְלוּכָה, פּוֹדֶה כַּהֲלָכָה, צַדִּיקָיו יֹאמְרוּ לוֹ: לְךָ וּלְךָ, לְךָ כִּי לְךָ, לְךָ אַף לְךָ, לְךָ יְיָ הַמַּמְלָכָה. כִּי לוֹ נָאֶה, כִּי לוֹ יָאֶה.

קָדוֹשׁ בִּמְלוּכָה, רַחוּם כַּהֲלָכָה, שִׁנְאַנָּיו יֹאמְרוּ לוֹ: לְךָ וּלְךָ, לְךָ כִּי לְךָ, לְךָ אַף לְךָ, לְךָ יְיָ הַמַּמְלָכָה. כִּי לוֹ נָאֶה, כִּי לוֹ יָאֶה.

תַּקִּיף בִּמְלוּכָה, תּוֹמֵךְ כַּהֲלָכָה, תְּמִימָיו יֹאמְרוּ לוֹ: לְךָ וּלְךָ, לְךָ כִּי לְךָ, לְךָ אַף לְךָ, לְךָ יְיָ הַמַּמְלָכָה. כִּי לוֹ נָאֶה, כִּי לוֹ יָאֶה.

אַדִּיר הוּא

אַדִּיר הוּא, יִבְנֶה בֵּיתוֹ בְּקָרוֹב, בִּמְהֵרָה בִּמְהֵרָה, בְּיָמֵינוּ בְּקָרוֹב. אֵל בְּנֵה, אֵל בְּנֵה, בְּנֵה בֵיתְךָ בְּקָרוֹב.

בָּחוּר הוּא, גָּדוֹל הוּא, דָּגוּל הוּא, יִבְנֶה בֵּיתוֹ בְּקָרוֹב, בִּמְהֵרָה בִּמְהֵרָה, בְּיָמֵינוּ בְּקָרוֹב. אֵל בְּנֵה, אֵל בְּנֵה, בְּנֵה בֵיתְךָ בְּקָרוֹב.

---

number seven is mystically associated with the natural world. Thus we have an allusion to the hope that the model of redemption that we have built on our *seder* night, which

Famous in kingship, truly glorious, His faithful sing to Him: "Yours, only Yours, O Lord, is the Majestic Kingdom." Beautiful praises are His due.

Guiltless in kingship, truly strong, His angels sing to Him: "Yours, only Yours, O Lord, is the Majestic Kingdom." Beautiful praises are His due.

Alone in kingship, truly powerful, His scholars sing to Him: "Yours, only Yours, O Lord, is the Majestic Kingdom." Beautiful praises are His due.

Commanding in kingship, truly revered, His near ones sing to Him: "Yours, only Yours, O Lord, is the Majestic Kingdom." Beautiful praises are His due.

Humble in kingship, truly redeeming, His righteous sing to Him: "Yours, only Yours, O Lord, is the Majestic Kingdom." Beautiful praises are His due.

Holy in kingship, truly merciful, His angels sing to Him: "Yours, only Yours, O Lord, is the Majestic Kingdom." Beautiful praises are His due.

Indomitable in kingship, truly sustaining, His innocent sing to Him: "Yours, only Yours, O Lord, is the Majestic Kingdom." Beautiful praises are His due.

ADIR HU

Mighty is He. May He soon rebuild His House. Rapidly, rapidly! Soon, in our days. God, rebuild; God, rebuild. Speedily rebuild Your House.

Choice is He. Great is He. Foremost is He. May He soon rebuild His House. Rapidly, rapidly! Soon, in our days. God, rebuild; God, rebuild. Speedily rebuild Your House.

---

closes with praise for the Redeemer, will go on to become a physical reality in our generation (Chagit Barnea, *A Celebration of the Haggadah,* The Women's Beit Midrash).

Glorious is He. Worthy is He. Faultless is He. Righteous is He. May He soon rebuild His House. Rapidly, rapidly! Soon, in our days. God, rebuild; God, rebuild. Speedily rebuild Your House.

Pure is He. One is He. Mighty is He. Wise is He. Sovereign is He. Awe-inspiring is He. Exalted is He. Powerful is He. Redeeming is He. Just is He. May He soon rebuild His House. Rapidly, rapidly! Soon, in our days. God, rebuild; God, rebuild. Speedily rebuild Your House.

Holy is He. Compassionate is He. Almighty is He. Omnipotent is He. May He soon rebuild His House. Rapidly, rapidly! Soon, in our days. God, rebuild; God, rebuild. Speedily rebuild Your House.

EHAD MI YODE'A?

Who knows one? I know one:

One is God of heaven and earth.

Who knows two? I know two:

Two stone tablets of the Law; One is God of heaven and earth.

Who knows three? I know three:

Three Patriarchs; Two stone tablets of the Law; One is God of heaven and earth.

Who knows four? I know four:

Four Matriarchs; Three Patriarchs; Two stone tablets of the Law; One is God of heaven and earth.

Who knows five? I know five:

חֲמִשָּׁה חֻמְשֵׁי תוֹרָה, אַרְבַּע אִמָּהוֹת, שְׁלֹשָׁה אָבוֹת, שְׁנֵי לֻחוֹת הַבְּרִית, אֶחָד אֱלֹהֵינוּ שֶׁבַּשָּׁמַיִם וּבָאָרֶץ.

שִׁשָּׁה מִי יוֹדֵעַ? שִׁשָּׁה אֲנִי יוֹדֵעַ:
שִׁשָּׁה סִדְרֵי מִשְׁנָה, חֲמִשָּׁה חֻמְשֵׁי תוֹרָה, אַרְבַּע אִמָּהוֹת, שְׁלֹשָׁה אָבוֹת, שְׁנֵי לֻחוֹת הַבְּרִית, אֶחָד אֱלֹהֵינוּ שֶׁבַּשָּׁמַיִם וּבָאָרֶץ.

שִׁבְעָה מִי יוֹדֵעַ? שִׁבְעָה אֲנִי יוֹדֵעַ:
שִׁבְעָה יְמֵי שַׁבַּתָּא, שִׁשָּׁה סִדְרֵי מִשְׁנָה, חֲמִשָּׁה חֻמְשֵׁי וָרָה, אַרְבַּע אִמָּהוֹת, שְׁלֹשָׁה אָבוֹת, שְׁנֵי לֻחוֹת הַבְּרִית, אֶחָד אֱלֹהֵינוּ שֶׁבַּשָּׁמַיִם וּבָאָרֶץ.

שְׁמוֹנָה מִי יוֹדֵעַ? שְׁמוֹנָה אֲנִי יוֹדֵעַ:
שְׁמוֹנָה יְמֵי מִילָה, שִׁבְעָה יְמֵי שַׁבַּתָּא, שִׁשָּׁה סִדְרֵי מִשְׁנָה, חֲמִשָּׁה חֻמְשֵׁי תוֹרָה, אַרְבַּע אִמָּהוֹת, שְׁלֹשָׁה אָבוֹת, שְׁנֵי לֻחוֹת הַבְּרִית, אֶחָד אֱלֹהֵינוּ שֶׁבַּשָּׁמַיִם וּבָאָרֶץ.

תִּשְׁעָה מִי יוֹדֵעַ? תִּשְׁעָה אֲנִי יוֹדֵעַ:
תִּשְׁעָה יַרְחֵי לֵדָה, שְׁמוֹנָה יְמֵי מִילָה, שִׁבְעָה יְמֵי שַׁבַּתָּא, שִׁשָּׁה סִדְרֵי מִשְׁנָה, חֲמִשָּׁה חֻמְשֵׁי תוֹרָה, אַרְבַּע אִמָּהוֹת, שְׁלֹשָׁה אָבוֹת, שְׁנֵי לֻחוֹת הַבְּרִית, אֶחָד אֱלֹהֵינוּ שֶׁבַּשָּׁמַיִם וּבָאָרֶץ.

עֲשָׂרָה מִי יוֹדֵעַ? עֲשָׂרָה אֲנִי יוֹדֵעַ:
עֲשָׂרָה דִבְּרַיָּא, תִּשְׁעָה יַרְחֵי לֵדָה, שְׁמוֹנָה יְמֵי מִילָה, שִׁבְעָה יְמֵי שַׁבַּתָּא, שִׁשָּׁה סִדְרֵי מִשְׁנָה, חֲמִשָּׁה חֻמְשֵׁי תוֹרָה, אַרְבַּע אִמָּהוֹת, שְׁלֹשָׁה אָבוֹת, שְׁנֵי לֻחוֹת הַבְּרִית, אֶחָד אֱלֹהֵינוּ שֶׁבַּשָּׁמַיִם וּבָאָרֶץ.

אַחַד עָשָׂר מִי יוֹדֵעַ? אַחַד עָשָׂר אֲנִי יוֹדֵעַ:
אַחַד עָשָׂר כּוֹכְבַיָּא, עֲשָׂרָה דִבְּרַיָּא, תִּשְׁעָה יַרְחֵי לֵדָה, שְׁמוֹנָה

Five the Books of Moses; Four Matriarchs; Three Patriarchs; Two stone tablets of the Law; One is God of heaven and earth.

Who knows six? I know six:

Six sections of Mishnah; Five the Books of Moses; Four Matriarchs; Three Patriarchs; Two stone tablets of the Law; One is God of heaven and earth.

Who knows seven? I know seven:

Seven days of the week; Six sections of Mishnah; Five the Books of Moses; Four Matriarchs; Three Patriarchs; Two stone tablets of the Law; One is God of heaven and earth.

Who knows eight? I know eight:

Eight days before the *brit milah*; Seven days of the week; Six sections of Mishnah; Five the Books of Moses; Four Matriarchs; Three Patriarchs; Two stone tablets of the Law; One is God of heaven and earth.

Who knows nine? I know nine:

Nine months to make a human child; Eight days before the *brit milah*; Seven days of the week; Six sections of Mishnah; Five the Books of Moses; Four Matriarchs; Three Patriarchs; Two stone tablets of the Law; One is God of heaven and earth.

Who knows ten? I know ten:

Ten, the Ten Commandments; Nine months to make a human child; Eight days before the *brit milah*; Seven days of the week; Six sections of Mishnah; Five the Books of Moses; Four Matriarchs; Three Patriarchs; Two stone tablets of the Law; One is God of heaven and earth.

Who knows eleven? I know eleven:

Eleven stars in Joseph's dream; Ten, the Ten Commandments; Nine months to make a human child; Eight days before the *brit milah*; Seven

יְמֵי מִילָה, שִׁבְעָה יְמֵי שַׁבַּתָּא, שִׁשָּׁה סִדְרֵי מִשְׁנָה, חֲמִשָּׁה חֻמְשֵׁי תוֹרָה, אַרְבַּע אִמָּהוֹת, שְׁלֹשָׁה אָבוֹת, שְׁנֵי לֻחוֹת הַבְּרִית, אֶחָד אֱלֹהֵינוּ שֶׁבַּשָּׁמַיִם וּבָאָרֶץ.

שְׁנֵים עָשָׂר מִי יוֹדֵעַ? שְׁנֵים עָשָׂר אֲנִי יוֹדֵעַ:
שְׁנֵים עָשָׂר שִׁבְטַיָּא, אַחַד עָשָׂר כּוֹכְבַיָּא, עֲשָׂרָה דִבְּרַיָּא, תִּשְׁעָה יַרְחֵי לֵדָה, שְׁמוֹנָה יְמֵי מִילָה, שִׁבְעָה יְמֵי שַׁבַּתָּא, שִׁשָּׁה סִדְרֵי מִשְׁנָה, חֲמִשָּׁה חֻמְשֵׁי תוֹרָה, אַרְבַּע אִמָּהוֹת, שְׁלֹשָׁה אָבוֹת, שְׁנֵי לֻחוֹת הַבְּרִית, אֶחָד אֱלֹהֵינוּ שֶׁבַּשָּׁמַיִם וּבָאָרֶץ.

שְׁלֹשָׁה עָשָׂר מִי יוֹדֵעַ? שְׁלֹשָׁה עָשָׂר אֲנִי יוֹדֵעַ:
שְׁלֹשָׁה עָשָׂר מִדַּיָּא, שְׁנֵים עָשָׂר שִׁבְטַיָּא, אַחַד עָשָׂר כּוֹכְבַיָּא, עֲשָׂרָה דִבְּרַיָּא, תִּשְׁעָה יַרְחֵי לֵדָה, שְׁמוֹנָה יְמֵי מִילָה, שִׁבְעָה יְמֵי שַׁבַּתָּא, שִׁשָּׁה סִדְרֵי מִשְׁנָה, חֲמִשָּׁה חֻמְשֵׁי תוֹרָה, אַרְבַּע אִמָּהוֹת, שְׁלֹשָׁה אָבוֹת, שְׁנֵי לֻחוֹת הַבְּרִית, אֶחָד אֱלֹהֵינוּ שֶׁבַּשָּׁמַיִם וּבָאָרֶץ.

חַד גַּדְיָא

חַד גַּדְיָא, חַד גַּדְיָא, דְּזַבִּין אַבָּא בִּתְרֵי זוּזֵי, חַד גַּדְיָא, חַד גַּדְיָא.

וְאָתָא שׁוּנְרָא, וְאָכְלָה לְגַדְיָא, דְּזַבִּין אַבָּא בִּתְרֵי זוּזֵי, חַד גַּדְיָא, חַד גַּדְיָא.

וְאָתָא כַלְבָּא, וְנָשַׁךְ לְשׁוּנְרָא, דְּאָכְלָה לְגַדְיָא, דְּזַבִּין אַבָּא בִּתְרֵי זוּזֵי, חַד גַּדְיָא, חַד גַּדְיָא.

וְאָתָא חוּטְרָא, וְהִכָּה לְכַלְבָּא, דְּנָשַׁךְ לְשׁוּנְרָא, דְּאָכְלָה לְגַדְיָא, דְּזַבִּין אַבָּא בִּתְרֵי זוּזֵי, חַד גַּדְיָא, חַד גַּדְיָא.

days of the week; Six sections of Mishnah; Five the Books of Moses; Four Matriarchs; Three Patriarchs; Two stone tablets of the Law; One is God of heaven and earth.

Who knows twelve? I know twelve:

Twelve tribes of Israel; Eleven stars in Joseph's dream; Ten, the Ten Commandments; Nine months to make a human child; Eight days before the *brit milah*; Seven days of the week; Six sections of Mishnah; Five the Books of Moses; Four Matriarchs; Three Patriarchs; Two stone tablets of the Law; One is God of heaven and earth.

Who knows thirteen? I know thirteen:

Thirteen attributes of God; Twelve tribes of Israel; Eleven stars in Joseph's dream; Ten, the Ten Commandments; Nine months to make a human child; Eight days before the *brit milah*; Seven days of the week; Six sections of Mishnah; Five the Books of Moses; Four Matriarchs; Three Patriarchs; Two stone tablets of the Law; One is God of heaven and earth.

HAD GADYA

One kid, One little kid, My father bought for two zuzim.

A cat passed by and ate the kid, One little kid, My father bought for two zuzim.

A dog arrived and bit the cat, that ate the kid, One little kid, My father bought for two zuzim.

A heavy stick then beat the dog, that bit the cat, that ate the kid, One little kid, My father bought for two zuzim.

וְאָתָא נוּרָא, וְשָׂרַף לְחֻטְרָא,דְּהִכָּה לְכַלְבָּא, דְּנָשַׁךְ לְשׁוּנְרָא, דְּאָכְלָה לְגַדְיָא, דְּזַבִּין אַבָּא בִּתְרֵי זוּזֵי, חַד גַּדְיָא, חַד גַּדְיָא.

וְאָתָא מַיָּא, וְכָבָה לְנוּרָא, דְּשָׂרַף לְחֻטְרָא, דְּהִכָּה לְכַלְבָּא, דְּנָשַׁךְ לְשׁוּנְרָא, דְּאָכְלָה לְגַדְיָא, דְּזַבִּין אַבָּא בִּתְרֵי זוּזֵי, חַד גַּדְיָא, חַד גַּדְיָא.

וְאָתָא תוֹרָא, וְשָׁתָא לְמַיָּא,דְּכָבָה לְנוּרָא, דְּשָׂרַף לְחֻטְרָא, דְּהִכָּה לְכַלְבָּא, דְּנָשַׁךְ לְשׁוּנְרָא, דְּאָכְלָה לְגַדְיָא, דְּזַבִּין אַבָּא בִּתְרֵי זוּזֵי, חַד גַּדְיָא, חַד גַּדְיָא.

וְאָתָא הַשּׁוֹחֵט, וְשָׁחַט לְתוֹרָא, דְּשָׁתָא לְמַיָּא, דְּכָבָה לְנוּרָא,דְּשָׂרַף לְחֻטְרָא, דְּהִכָּה לְכַלְבָּא, דְּנָשַׁךְ לְשׁוּנְרָא, דְּאָכְלָה לְגַדְיָא, דְּזַבִּין אַבָּא בִּתְרֵי זוּזֵי, חַד גַּדְיָא, חַד גַּדְיָא.

וְאָתָא מַלְאַךְ הַמָּוֶת, וְשָׁחַט לְשׁוֹחֵט, דְּשָׁחַט לְתוֹרָא, דְּשָׁתָא לְמַיָּא, דְּכָבָה לְנוּרָא, דְּשָׂרַף לְחֻטְרָא, דְּהִכָּה לְכַלְבָּא, דְּנָשַׁךְ לְשׁוּנְרָא, דְּאָכְלָה לְגַדְיָא,דְּזַבִּין אַבָּא בִּתְרֵי זוּזֵי, חַד גַּדְיָא, חַד גַּדְיָא.

וְאָתָא הַקָּדוֹשׁ בָּרוּךְ הוּא, וְשָׁחַט לְמַלְאַךְ הַמָּוֶת, דְּשָׁחַט לְשׁוֹחֵט, דְּשָׁחַט לְתוֹרָא, דְּשָׁתָא לְמַיָּא, דְּכָבָה לְנוּרָא,דְּשָׂרַף לְחֻטְרָא, דְּהִכָּה לְכַלְבָּא, דְּנָשַׁךְ לְשׁוּנְרָא, דְּאָכְלָה לְגַדְיָא, דְּזַבִּין אַבָּא בִּתְרֵי זוּזֵי, חַד גַּדְיָא, חַד גַּדְיָא.

A fire burned the heavy stick, that beat the dog, that bit the cat, that ate the kid, One little kid, My father bought for two zuzim.

Water doused the fire, that burned the stick, that beat the dog that bit the cat, that ate the kid, One little kid, My father bought for two zuzim.

An ox drank all, that water up, that doused the fire, that burned the stick, that beat the dog, that bit the cat, that ate the kid, One little kid, My father bought for two zuzim.

A butcher slaughtered the same ox, that drank the water, that doused the fire, that burned the stick, that beat the dog, that bit the cat, that ate the kid, One little kid, My father bought for two zuzim.

The Angel of Death took off the butcher who slaughtered the ox, that drank the water, that doused the fire, that burned the stick, that beat the dog, that bit the cat, that ate the kid, One little kid, My father bought for two zuzim.

Then the Holy One Blessed be He killed the Angel of Death, who took off the butcher who slaughtered the ox, that drank the water, that doused the fire, that burned the stick, that beat the dog, that bit the cat, that ate the kid, One little kid, My father bought for two zuzim.

ABOUT THE AUTHOR

JOEL B. WOLOWELSKY is Dean of the Faculty at the Yeshivah of Flatbush, where he teaches math and Jewish Philosophy. He is associate editor of *Tradition*, the journal of Orthodox Jewish thought published by the Rabbinical Council of America, and the series *MeOtzar HoRav: Selected Writings of Rabbi Joseph B. Soloveitchik*. Dr. Wolowelsky is a member of the Professional Advisory Board of the Bar Ilan University Lookstein Center for Jewish Education in the Diaspora, ATID (Academy for Torah Initiatives and Directions), and the Pardes Educators Program. His other books include *Women, Jewish Law and Modernity: New Opportunities in a Post-feminist Age*, and *Women and the Study of Torah*, both published by Ktav.